Taken up into heaven

Taken up into heaven —

the ascension of Christ

Derek Thomas

EVANGELICAL PRESS

EVANGELICAL PRESS
12 Wooler Street, Darlington, Co. Durham, DL1 1RQ, England

© Evangelical Press 1996
First published 1996

British Library Cataloguing in Publication Data available

ISBN 0 85234 386 8

Printed and Bound in Great Britain by
Creative Print and Design Wales, Ebbw Vale, Gwent

To
GEOFF THOMAS
to whom I owe so much

Contents

		Page
Foreword by Professor J. Ligon Duncan		9
Preface		13
1.	The ascension of Jesus	17
2.	'Coming home': Jesus presenting himself before his Father in heaven	37
3.	Jesus receives a crown	51
4.	Pouring out the Holy Spirit	67
5.	Distributing gifts to the church	84
6.	Jesus the home-maker	97
7.	The ministry of sympathy and intercession	112
8.	Watching for the return of our Lord	129
Notes		137

Foreword

The wise old Reformed theologians of the seventeenth century have taught us that there are three stages in the exaltation of Christ: the resurrection (Rom. 1:4), the ascension (Luke 24:51) and the session at the Father's right hand (Heb. 1:3). This exaltation was essential to the fulfilment of the covenant of redemption. Divine justice demanded the exaltation of Christ, according to the promises of God to him in his capacity as the mediator of his people. He had to be raised (and thus vindicated), to be taken up (and thus exalted), to be enthroned (and thus established in his eternal reign).

His exaltation, furthermore, served to reveal and apply all the benefits of his completed work of redemption to those chosen by God, that is, all who are in Christ. When in the Scriptures we see him seated in glory, we are reminded of the heavenly Father's acceptance of (and, indeed, delight in) his saving work, and thus the Father's acceptance of us, in him. When in the Scriptures we see him seated in glory, we are also reminded that he rules the world for the benefit of his people, and from the right hand he sends the Holy Spirit to apply to the Father's children all the blessings which flow from his redeeming work.

In the ascension, the Son of God in flesh, the incarnate Second Person of the blessed Trinity, was raised locally,

visibly and bodily from earth to 'the third heaven' (2 Cor. 12:2;
Heb. 4:14; 7:26; Eph. 4:10), that is, into the very presence of
God, into the heaven of heavens. This was neither a mere
obscuring of his visible presence, nor a divinization of his
humanity (his human nature did not thus become ubiquitous,
as some like to say), but a real translation of his resurrected
human body to the throne of God, where it will dwell until the
great Day of Judgement. Hence, though our Lord is present
with us by his grace and through his Holy Spirit, he is no longer
physically present with us. For this, we must await the reunion.

While much has been written of the resurrection of Christ,
and much thought has been devoted to his heavenly session,
comparatively little has been said about the significance of the
ascension. This is a shame, not only because Christ's ascension is a scriptural teaching, and not only because it is a truth
of credal status, but also because this doctrine is filled with
supreme comfort for all believers. How, one may rightly
ask, can such a doctrine give us comfort? There are many
biblical answers to that question which one will learn in this
good book, but the following come readily to mind:

1. Christ's ascension serves as confirmation of the
fulfilment and efficacy of the covenant of grace. In
Christ's ascension, the Father shows to all Christ's
people what he will one day show to the whole world
(Heb. 8:1-2; 1 Tim. 3:16; Phil. 2:9-11).

2. Christ's ascension opens heaven up to his people.
He is our forerunner there, as he was in the resurrection,
and has ascended there to prepare the place for us (John
14:2-3).

3. Christ's ascension into his heavenly heritage guar-
antees the future glories held in reserve for his brethren.
By his entrance into the Father's presence he serves as
surety for our eternal inheritance (Heb. 9:15); indeed

Paul tells us that we are already 'seated with him' (Eph. 2:6).

4. Christ's ascension was necessary for his pouring out of the Holy Spirit upon his people (John 16:7). From his exalted position at the Father's right hand and in his ascended splendour Christ dispenses his Holy Spirit as Comforter, Counsellor, pledge and down-payment.

5. Finally, Christ's ascension draws our hearts to him and our desires to communion with him in paradise.

No man can *love* both God and mammon any more than one can *serve* both God and mammon (Matt. 6:24). The world allures us with its temporal charms and ephemeral promises, but in Christ's ascension our hearts have been set on things above (Col. 3:1-3).

Oh, yes, there is a balm of encouragement stored up in the truth of the ascension — for home-makers, for professionals, for students, for ministers, for children, for adults! All Christians have an interest in our Lord's ascension, and all of us should be interested to learn of this great doctrine from God's holy Word. Do you wonder if sin will finally triumph over humanity? Consider the ascension. By it, as John Duncan said a century ago, 'The dust of the earth sits on the throne of heaven.' The fact that God's Son has ascended and even now sits, *in our flesh,* at the right hand proves the ultimate glorification of all redeemed humanity! Does a believer wish proof that Christ's work of active and passive obedience has met the standards of divine holiness? Look at the ascension. In it Christ has been shown to be the redeeming Son of God with power. Are you downcast? Have you physical maladies that have taxed your constitution or threatened your life? Are there heartbreaks in home and family life, and seemingly none to help bear your burden? Are you living in the valley, out of the sight of the mount of the Lord? Remember the ascension. The bodily translation of our Saviour from earth to heaven is the foreshadowing of our future experience. As Duncan Rankin has put it, 'In our flesh we are oppressed. In our flesh we shall see God.'

Dear reader, in this subjective era of 'how-to' and 'self-help' and technique, we need desperately to lay hold of the great objective truths of Christianity: the nature and attributes of God, the doctrine of the holy Trinity, revelation, incarnation, redemption, atonement, justification, adoption, the divine creation of the church, the Second Coming and others. We contribute absolutely nothing to these realities and are not called on by God to contribute anything to them — only to stand and behold the salvation of the Lord. We need to sit under these truths, and feed on them, grow in them, be made strong in them. The ascension is one such neglected truth.

It is my prayer that you will, in your study of this book, learn of him with whom we have to do and be given yet more cause to praise him. Your guide, Derek Thomas, is a faithful and wise shepherd of souls, and a man of the Book. He is also an admired friend and older brother in the Lord. May his labours serve to feed your soul, strengthen your mind, encourage your walk and woo you to Christ, your ascended Bridegroom.

J. Ligon Duncan

J. Ligon Duncan was formerly the John R. Richardson Professor of Systematic Theology at the Reformed Theological Seminary, Jackson, Mississippi, USA, and is now Senior Pastor of the First Presbyterian Church, Jackson, Mississippi.

Preface

Christian preaching and teaching rightly give emphasis to the death of Jesus Christ. The events of Calvary are of supreme importance and without them we are lost and condemned. Emphasis has also been given to the resurrection of Jesus Christ, accounting as it does for the claim of Jesus to be both Saviour and Lord. If the tomb is still occupied, we are again lost and condemned. For forty days following his resurrection, Jesus made several appearances in his resurrected body which were intended to convince his doubting disciples that all was well; but these phenomena were always meant to be of temporary duration. He was on his way home. Indeed, there is every reason to think that he made several visits home during these forty days. These return visits to earth grew less frequent; the time came for him to go home for good. Such a departure needed to be decisive and spectacular, something on a par with the resurrection itself. Such an event was the ascension.

Two things were signalled by the ascension: Jesus went up — thereby giving the clearest possible indication of his higher status and exaltation; Jesus disappeared into a cloud — something which in biblical terms was meant to signify his reception into God's near presence. Quite simply, the ascension conveyed that Jesus went home to be with his Father in heaven. Nothing could be more central to the ministry of the Son of

God than this culminating act of triumph. It deserves to be told over and over again, firstly because it is biblical and the church ought never to underplay what the Bible stresses; and secondly, because so much flows down to us as a direct consequence of Christ's rising into heaven. Not least is the New Covenant ministry of the Holy Spirit — Christ's 'Vicar', as Tertullian arrestingly termed the Third Person of the Trinity. For an age which craves relevance, the ascension is a doctrine every Christian should take to heart and ponder with affection. 'It is an article of faith,' wrote Caspar Olevianus (one of the original framers of the *Heidelberg Catechism*), 'that [Jesus] ascended from earth into heaven, where He is carrying out the other part of His priesthood, His appearing in heaven for us before the throne of God.'[1] Jesus appears in heaven for us!

Jesus is no more 'down here', but 'up there'! We are meant to focus, you and I, on heaven. Time and again, the New Testament urges us to catch a glimpse of 'things above' (Eph. 1:21; Phil. 2:6-11; Col. 3:1; Heb. 7:26; 12:1-2, etc.). Our Christian lives are paralysed because we fail to see Jesus, as he now is, risen and exalted. Our vision is too earth-bound, too restricted. The doctrine of the ascension forces us to lift up our heads and look up. Too often we are like those two miserable souls on the Emmaus road, searching for answers on the floor. What we need is someone to come alongside us and show us that Jesus is alive and reigning from a throne in heaven. The course of our lives, and of this world in which we live, is already mapped out. Jesus Christ is now at God's right hand, actively interceding on our behalf, ensuring that every facet of this plan be fulfilled.

The ascension of Christ is 'one of the chief points of our faith,' wrote John Calvin,[2] and he was right. In studying this theme we shall have to focus on heaven where he now resides. Thinking about our Saviour in heaven is never dull, always rewarding. It was one of the last things Jesus spoke about before his death. He wanted to assure his disciples that one day they, too, would be with him, sharing in the glory of his immediate presence. It was meant as a fillip to their flagging faith. My aim in writing this book is singular: to help focus our gaze on Jesus in his glory. There is no more rewarding occupation than this.

> I view the Lamb in his own light,
> Whom angels dimly see,
> And gaze, transported with the sight,
> To all eternity.
>
> Charles Wesley (1707-88)[3]

Everything that I would wish to say by way of an introduction, and more, has been said by my friend, Ligon Duncan, who has kindly agreed to write the foreword to this volume. I urge you to read what he has to say, for in a few lines he has summarized what is most essential for us to know. It is the heart that makes the theologian, said Anselm, and if we are to make sense of the ascension, we must allow it first to affect our hearts — humbling and shaping them into organs of worship and wonder before the majesty of Christ. As a teacher of systematic theology, Ligon Duncan is convinced of this, too.

I trust that what is written in these pages affects your minds and your hearts. If it causes some of the Lord's people to live this life with greater patience, drawing from the resources of Christ's current ministry from his throne in heaven; if it causes some of you to look up, rather than down, it will have fulfilled its purpose.

Once again, thanks are due to the folk at Stranmillis Evangelical Presbyterian Church in Belfast who heard most of what is written in sermonic form. Their encouragement was incalculable. Since writing this book I have, in the Lord's providence, been relocated to Jackson, Mississippi. Looking back over seventeen years of ministry in Stranmillis EPC, I am more than ever grateful to the gracious providence that brought me in touch with these kind and godly folk.

My wife and children are amongst those whom I count most dear in this world, and without their help I would not have been able to do for my Lord what I have.

I am also grateful once again to my publishers for their valuable efforts in seeking to purify and purge these pages of that which ought not to appear.

It is time, then, to turn to the ascension.

Derek Thomas

Reformed Theological Seminary,
Jackson, Mississippi, USA
November 1996

1.
The ascension of Jesus

One may imagine the story of a father who welcomes his son home from war. There were times when it looked as though the son might not make it through the battle. The hostility had been fierce and the marks of battle now lie permanently etched on his body. There were times when communication had not been possible; but now, there is joy as they greet one another again. This is the story of redemption, as Jesus, God's only Son, returns from his battle against sin and death to embrace his Father in heaven. This is what the ascension is principally about.

On the cross, Jesus 'disarmed the powers and authorities' (Col. 2:15), shaking off and discarding the evil powers that clung to him as one does a garment for which one has no more use (the middle voice of the Greek verb translated as 'to disarm' would seem to suggest this). Perhaps the thought is otherwise: that Jesus stripped the evil powers of their assumed authority, demoting them of their pretentious claims to position and privilege (it is possible to read the verb in this way). Having done so, Jesus 'made a public spectacle of them, triumphing over them by the cross', in much the same way as an ancient general might march through his home city, holding aloft the booty from victories in battle against a mighty foe. Jesus, the Mighty Conqueror, has returned — in triumph!

Biographical accounts of the life of Jesus Christ usually begin with his birth and end, not with his death, as might at first be supposed, but with his resurrection. The ascension is hardly mentioned, and one can understand why. Three reasons seem to account for it.

First, *the Gospels hardly make any mention of the ascension at all.* Mark mentions it, but the reference falls in a passage which has been greatly disputed: 'After the Lord Jesus had spoken to them, he was taken up into heaven and he sat at the right hand of God' (Mark 16:19). Luke makes a similar reference, brief and to the point: 'When he had led them out to the vicinity of Bethany, he lifted up his hands and blessed them. While he was blessing them, he left them and was taken up into heaven' (Luke 24:50-51). That an event of such magnitude should be so singularly bypassed by the other Gospel writers need not surprise us unduly.

If asked to list those events in the life and ministry of Jesus Christ which are of greatest import, most of us would place the virgin birth somewhere near the top. Yet only two of the Gospel writers make any mention of it (Matt. 1:18-25; Luke 1:26-56; 2:4-7). And the apostle Paul omits any reference to it whatsoever. Despite this, the virgin birth has found its way into standard statements of fundamental doctrine, as the Apostles' Creed testifies: 'I believe in God, the Father Almighty, Maker of heaven and earth: And in Jesus Christ, his only Son, our Lord; who was conceived by the Holy Ghost, born of the virgin Mary...' Similarly, the creed ties in Christ's resurrection directly to the ascension and heavenly reign: 'The third day he rose again from the dead; he ascended into heaven and sits on the right hand of God the Father Almighty.'

A second reason explaining the lack of emphasis on the ascension is *the primary importance given to the resurrection in the New Testament.* When Christians desire to demonstrate Jesus' deity, validate his teaching, attest to the completion of his work of atonement for sin, or confirm his present cosmic dominion and his coming appearance as Judge, they invariably point to the resurrection. In addition, when they seek assurance of the personal pardon, presence and power of God in their lives, or a guarantee of their own personal re-embodiment by resurrection in the world to come, they instinctively point to Jesus' resurrection. And in so doing they echo the apostle, for amongst the doctrines of 'first importance' in his apostolic preaching, he enumerates: 'that Christ died for our sins according to the Scriptures, that he was buried, that he was raised on the third day according to the Scriptures' (1 Cor. 15:3-4).

It is no exaggeration to state that Christianity rests on the certainty of Jesus' resurrection as a space-time occurrence in history. All four Gospels focus on the empty tomb and the various accounts of resurrection appearances. 'If Christ has not been raised, our preaching is useless and so is your faith' (1 Cor. 15:14). To emphasize the ascension at the expense of the resurrection would be a fatal error of judgement. Rather, we should view the resurrection and the ascension as of a piece. The moment Jesus left the tomb he was on his way to the Father's right hand. The resurrection began what the ascension was to complete: Jesus' return to the glory he knew before (cf. John 17:1,5).

A third reason for the lack of emphasis on the ascension is that *for many talk of a body rising into the air is unbelievable*! The idea of someone physically rising into the sky has drawn ridicule from many quarters. Some have felt that it simply makes Jesus to be some kind of primitive cosmonaut! It has been pointed out, for example, that Luke gives only a tacit account of Christ's withdrawal in his Gospel, amounting to a summary statement devoid of any reference to a physical ascent into the sky: 'While he was blessing them, he left them and was taken up into heaven' (Luke 24:51). Later, when

composing his second volume, the Acts of the Apostles, Luke
(so it is argued) embellished the story adding to the account
that Jesus rose into the sky. This has led some to the conclusion
that what we have in Acts is not to be taken literally. It is Luke's
vivid use of word-pictures illustrating that Jesus went to
heaven (which, in the thought-world of the day, was 'up there',
'beyond the sky'). Evidence for this has been cited in terms of
supposed contradictions between the account in Luke's Gospel and that in Acts (also by Luke!). Our task in reading the
Bible is to 'demythologize' such accounts, removing these
'embellishments' and 'contradictions', thus finding the core
teaching — namely, that Jesus went to heaven.

Such, then, are the three main objections to the ascension.
What are we to make of them? Of course, a predisposition to
accept the authority and reliability of the Scriptures leads us to
read the ascension as a literal and necessary aspect of Christ's
exaltation to the Father's side. What precisely are the biblical
data relating to the ascension?

The biblical data — the Old Testament

The theological expectations of the early Christians were
formed by the teaching of the Old Testament. In page after
page, they understood God to be preparing them for the
coming of Messiah. The Old Testament spoke of Christ: his
coming, his death, his exaltation to God's right hand. As
Augustine said, 'The New is in the Old concealed; the Old is
by the New revealed.' This was how Jesus himself understood
it. On the Friday afternoon they had taken Jesus down from the
cross, as dead as a man can be. On the Sunday afternoon he
walked with two others along the road that led to Emmaus. He
had broken through the barrier of death. During the course of
his seven-mile walk he engaged in a lengthy Bible study,

pointing out the various passages in the Old Testament that had spoken about his coming, his mission, his death and presumably his ascension (Luke 24:13-35). Which passages did he select? We are not told, but several relating to the ascension would seem to have been likely.

To begin with, a collection of psalms have been consistently interpreted by the New Testament church as signalling the ascension and consequent session of Christ at God's right hand.

Psalm 2, particularly verses 7-9, is cited often in the New Testament (Matt. 3:17; 17:5; Acts 13:33; Heb. 1:1-5; 2 Peter 1:17; Rev. 12:5; 19:15):

> I will proclaim the decree of the LORD:
> He said to me, 'You are my Son;
>> today I have become your Father.
> Ask of me,
>> and I will make the nations your inheritance,
>> the ends of the earth your possession.
> You will rule them with an iron sceptre ;
>> you will dash them to pieces like pottery.'

This is one of the royal psalms where the anointed of the LORD, the Messiah, speaks to announce his relationship to the LORD. Of particular significance is the use made of these words by the Father at Jesus' baptism and transfiguration (Matt. 3:17; 17:5; 2 Peter 1:17). There is to be no end to Jesus' rule.

Psalm 8 contains a reference to the subjugation of creation to the rule of man at the end of the age:

> You made him ruler over the works of your hands;
>> you put everything under his feet
>>> (Ps. 8:6).

The psalm is cited by Paul in 1 Corinthians 15:27-28 to suggest that God, the Father, has already put all things under Jesus' feet. What will be subjected to man at the end of the age is already subject to Christ now. It is a depiction of the current rule of Christ over creation.

Psalm 68 is also cited as proof of Jesus' ascension (Eph. 4:8).

> When you ascended on high,
>   you led captives in your train;
>   you received gifts from men,
> even from the rebellious—
>   that you, O LORD God, might dwell there
>
>   (Ps. 68:18).

In its original setting, the psalm probably recalled the ascending of the ark of the covenant (as a symbol of God's presence amongst his people) from the house of Obed-Edom the Gittite to its final resting-place on Mount Zion in Jerusalem (2 Sam. 6). It celebrates the progressive nature of God's rule over his enemies as he takes his place on the throne of Jerusalem. But in Christ a far greater ascension is depicted. In this respect, Psalm 68 is similar to the way some verses of Psalm 24 have been understood:

> Lift up your heads, O you gates;
>   be lifted up, you ancient doors,
>   that the King of glory may come in.
> Who is this King of glory?
>   The LORD strong and mighty,
>   the LORD mighty in battle.
> Lift up your heads, O you gates;
>   lift them up, you ancient doors,
>   that the King of glory may come in.

Who is he, this King of glory?
    The LORD Almighty—
    he is the King of glory

(Ps. 24:7-10).

This psalm also depicts the bringing of the ark into Jerusalem, and the ascent of Mount Zion is depicted as the culmination of the journey that began in Egypt. The church has always seen it as a reference to Christ's triumph. Thus, Christopher Wordsworth's hymn:

See, the Conqueror mounts in triumph;
See the King in royal state,
Riding on the clouds, his chariot,
To his heav'nly palace gate:
Hark! The choirs of angel voices
Joyful Allelujas sing
And the portals high are lifted
To receive their heav'nly King.

Who is this that comes in glory,
With the trump of jubilee?
Lord of battles, God of armies,
He has gained the victory;
He who on the cross did suffer,
He who from the grave arose,
He has vanquished sin and Satan,
He by death has spoiled his foes.

Thou hast raised our human nature
In the clouds to God's right hand;
There we sit in heav'nly places,
There with thee in glory stand:
Jesus reigns adored by angels,

Man with God is on the throne;
Mighty Lord, in thine ascension
We by faith behold our own.

Another psalm is Psalm 110, particularly verses 1 and 4:

The LORD says to my Lord:
    'Sit at my right hand
until I make your enemies
    a footstool for your feet' ...
The LORD has sworn
    and will not change his mind:
'You are a priest for ever,
    in the order of Melchizedek.'

David is speaking of the enthronement of a future king over
Israel, but in doing so alludes to one who is co-regent with the
God of Israel! The New Testament frequently sees this as a
reference to Jesus (Matt. 22:44; Mark 12:36; Luke 20:42-43;
Acts 2:34-35; 1 Cor. 15:25; Heb. 5:6; 6:20; 7:17,21; 10:12).
The future King of Israel is one who will sit at God's right
hand.

The biblical data — the New Testament

We have already noted the references in Mark and Luke, but
neither gives a description of the event itself; they merely
report its occurrence. The ascension is also referred to indi-
rectly in many other parts of Scripture. John records in the
upper room discourse Jesus' insistence on the need for him to
'go away'. He knows that his hour has come when he must go
to the Father (John 13:3; 14:28; 14:2). He says to the disciples,
'Where I am going, you cannot come' (John 13:33) and to the

Jews, 'You will look for me, but you will not find me; and where I am, you cannot come' (John 7:34). Jesus insisted that 'It is for your good that I am going away' (John 16:7). His going away will enable him to prepare a place for his disciples (John 14:2) and to send the Holy Spirit as their Helper (John 16:7-10).

Jesus insisted that the time was coming when he would be 'glorified' (John 12:23). Clearly, he was preparing them for a time when he would no longer be with them in the same sense as he had been. This explains Jesus' first conversation with Mary Magdalene after the resurrection. Seeing him alive from the dead, Mary was overcome with a desire to embrace him. But Jesus said to her, 'Do not hold on to me, for I have not yet returned to the Father. Go instead to my brothers and tell them, "I am returning to my Father and your Father, to my God and your God"' (John 20:17). These words are often misunderstood. It sounds like a cold-hearted dismissal of an emotionally charged woman. But Jesus was saying nothing of the sort. Instead, he was re-educating her. She must not cling to him any more for he must leave her and go to his Father in heaven. She must learn to fellowship with a Saviour she can no longer see or touch.

It is Luke, in the Acts of the Apostles, who expands on the nature of the ascension, describing it in a vivid and unforgettable way: 'After he said this, he was taken up before their very eyes, and a cloud hid him from their sight' (Acts 1:9). There are several features which need clarification.

1. Luke relates in his Gospel (volume 1 of the *Life and Times of Jesus Christ,* the Acts being volume 2) that Jesus 'was taken up into heaven' (Luke 24:51). This creates a problem, for Luke records a series of resurrection appearances, beginning on the day of resurrection, without suggesting in any way that forty days elapse

before the ascension takes place. When Luke comes to write the Acts account, he expands on the details of the event, explaining that the appearances did not take place on the same day but were in fact spread over a period of some five to six weeks, after which Jesus rose to be with his Father in heaven. It takes some credibility to assume that the same author could get things so terribly wrong as to suggest an ascension on the same day as the resurrection in his Gospel, and another ascension some forty days later in the Acts. And this from an author who claimed, in his first volume, to have investigated everything carefully with the aid of eyewitness accounts and painstaking research! (Luke 1:1-4). Luke is describing the same event in both volumes.

2. There are certain details which appear in one account and not in the other. This is not uncommon in the Bible when the same incident is being retold. Often the explanation is theological: sometimes, in the interests of stressing a particular point, the author selects an aspect of the story to illustrate this. Thus, in Luke's Gospel account, he mentions that, prior to the ascension, Jesus lifted up his hands to bless the disciples. That makes theological sense, for one of Luke's purposes at the close of the Gospel account is to prepare the disciples for mission: training camp is over and field service is about to begin. They need to be clothed with power from on high, and in a symbolic gesture Jesus raises his hands in customary fashion signalling blessing. The cross, far from destroying the purposes of God, actually fulfils it. They need not be disillusioned, as the two on the Emmaus road had been.

Following the blessing (and the ascension) the disciples returned to Jerusalem full of worship, praise and great joy. Everything speaks of anticipation. When Luke opens his second volume he wants to stress something else: not so much the need of the disciples for spiritual encouragement (the blessing), but their need of divine *power*. Jesus is received up into a cloud which, as we shall see, is representative of the glory of God. The one who blesses is received into the glory-presence of God. As they await their orders for mission, what they see in the ascension of Jesus is a symbol of power. Far from contradicting himself, Luke complements the accounts, emphasizing different aspects to suit his purpose in retelling the story.

3. Another discrepancy has been alleged, regarding the location of the ascension. The Acts relates the ascension from the Mount of Olives, which is correctly said to be a Sabbath day's walk from Jerusalem (just over a thousand metres), whilst the Gospel account tells us that it took place in the 'vicinity of Bethany' (Luke 24:50). Bethany is possibly as much as three miles away from Jerusalem, but Luke does not say that the ascension took place from Bethany, but only in the *direction* of Bethany and since the Mount of Olives is in that direction it is perfectly understandable that by the time Luke came to write Acts the exact spot had become known and talked about to a greater degree of accuracy than it had before. The Mount of Olives became associated with Jesus' ministry in such a way that folk now wished to recall the very spot. There is no contradiction.

What did the disciples see?

Luke makes a great deal in his account of eyewitnesses; he wants us to understand that the ascension was really quite literal. The cumulative stress is compelling: 'He was taken up

before their very eyes, and a cloud hid him *from their sight.*
They were *looking intently up* into the sky as he was going,
when suddenly two men dressed in white stood beside them.
"Men of Galilee," they said, "why do you stand here *looking*
into the sky? This same Jesus, who has been taken from you
into heaven, will come back in the same way you have *seen*
him go into heaven"' (Acts 1:9-11, emphasis added).   Five
times Luke mentions that the ascension was something that
could be seen. In precisely the same way as the incarnation,
death and resurrection of Christ, the ascension was a physical
act in space and time. Eyewitnesses, on whom Luke has
depended as sources for his writings (cf. Luke 1:2), could (and
did) verify its occurrence. The apostles were themselves to
become eyewitnesses, giving testimony to what they had seen
of the two things that marked the beginning and end of Jesus'
earthly, public ministry — his baptism by John and the
ascension from the Mount of Olives (Acts 1:22).

We are led to believe that the disciples were not expecting
the ascension. In one sense they ought to have been. We have
already noted the number of occasions Jesus spoke of his
'going away'. But as Peter was to make clear in his Pentecost
sermon, the Old Testament, and Psalm 110 in particular, ought
to have prepared them for it. What we have of Peter's sermon
is only a summary, but in a few short verses Peter mentions the
resurrection, exaltation and the pouring forth of the Holy Spirit
(Acts 2:32-33). Alluding to Psalm 110, he cites in particular
the verse, 'The Lord said to my Lord: "Sit at my right hand..."'
This, argues Peter, was not said of David, for 'David did not
ascend to heaven' (Acts 2:34; cf. Ps. 110:1). In a similar way,
Paul argues the ascension of Christ from Psalm 68: 'What does
"he ascended" mean except that he also descended to the
lower, earthly regions? He who descended is the very one who
ascended higher than all the heavens, in order to fill the whole
universe' (Eph. 4:9-10).

What did the disciples expect?

The question put to Jesus just before his ascension revealed the confusion in their minds: 'So when they met together, they asked him, "Lord, are you at this time going to restore the kingdom to Israel?"' (Acts 1:6). Calvin remarks on this verse: 'There are as many errors in this question as words.'[1] Three things in particular should be noted:

1. The restoration of the kingdom

The disciples were confused about the *nature* of the kingdom. Nor were they alone. Great prominence is given in the Gospels to the fact that the focus of Jesus' preaching was the kingdom of God. In the Sermon on the Mount he made it the focus of every Christian's attention: 'But seek first his kingdom and his righteousness, and all these things will be given to you as well' (Matt. 6:33). His very first words recorded in the Gospels relate to the kingdom: 'Repent, for the kingdom of heaven is near' (Matt. 3:2). Luke records that the theme of Jesus' ministry after the resurrection also related to the kingdom of God (Acts 1:3). Despite this, confusion reigned as to the nature of the kingdom that Jesus had in mind. There is some evidence that the disciples, like the Pharisees and Pilate, believed the kingdom to be essentially political in nature (Acts 1:4-7; cf. Luke 17:21, where Jesus tells the Pharisees that 'The kingdom of God is within you'; and John 18:36, where Jesus tells Pilate, who believed he knew a thing or two about kingdoms, 'My kingdom is not of this world'). God's kingdom is not so much a domain but a dominion, not so much a territory but rule: God's rule in the hearts and lives of those who repent and believe the good news of the gospel. The Acts of the Apostles relate the expansion of God's kingdom in the lives of thousands of men and women who come to faith in Jesus

Christ and make the invisible kingdom visible through faithful
Christian living, which at its heart contains good news of
righteousness, peace and joy in the Holy Spirit (Rom. 14:17).
The kingdom comes not so much by restoration, but 'regener-
ation' (*apoktastasis,* Acts 3:21).

2. The place of Israel in God's purposes

It is not difficult to appreciate why it was that the disciples
believed that the kingdom essentially involved the nation of
Israel: 'Lord, are you at this time going to restore the kingdom
to *Israel*?' God had chosen this nation, not any other, to be the
vehicle of his redemptive purposes. The two disciples on the
road to Emmaus looked to all the world like disillusioned folk.
And why? Because they had thought Jesus would have redeemed Israel (Luke 24:21). The focus of their thoughts was
confined to the land of Israel. But Pentecost would change all
that. They were to be witnesses 'in Jerusalem, and in all Judea
and Samaria, and to the ends of the earth' (Acts 1:8). The
ascension spelled out mission to the world.

3. The arrival of the kingdom

The disciples also expected the kingdom to come *immediately.*
The resurrection had reignited their hopes that the occupying
forces of Rome might at last be evicted. But that was not to be;
it was not the principal aim in the establishment of the
kingdom of God.

Christians have often been confused whenever the New
Testament refers to the kingdom of God. It is often forgotten
that the last days have already dawned in the first coming of
Jesus Christ. The world to come is already pressing upon us;
these are the *last days* (Heb. 1:2). Jesus Christ appeared 'at the
end of the ages' to atone for sin (Heb. 9:26). Even now,

through faith in the risen and ascended Christ, we have 'tasted the goodness of the word of God and the powers of the coming age' (Heb. 6:5). When Jesus rose into heaven (symbolized by the glory-cloud), heaven also came down to earth. The tension between what is true *now* and what is *yet to be* has often been likened to the days following the Normandy landings on the shores of Europe and the ultimate cessation of hostilities, that is to say, between D-day and V-day of the Second World War. D-day was the decisive battle. The outcome of the war was never in doubt after that. That is not to say that hostilities ceased immediately. They did not! Indeed, some of the fiercest battles were fought during this interval. But V-day was always in sight, even when the battle raged at its worst, and the prospect of it kept the soldiers enduring the strife. Jesus' rising into the glory-cloud was a signal that his servant-work had been done; the victory had been won. The eventual course of history was certain.

Clouds of glory

If Jesus had to correct them as to the nature, extent and arrival of the kingdom, he also instructed them by ascending up into a cloud! Clouds have a special significance when it comes to the Scriptures. In the Old Testament clouds often accompanied the glory and majesty of God. Israel was led through the wilderness by a cloud by day and fiery pillar by night. At the dedication of the tabernacle in the wilderness, the cloud of glory, the *shekinah*, covered the place and thereafter dwelt above the ark of the covenant in the Holy of Holies. At the transfiguration, a voice was heard to speak to Jesus from out of a cloud, saying, 'This is my Son...' And clouds accompany the mode of Jesus' second coming: 'Look, he is coming with the clouds, and every eye will see him... Amen' (Rev. 1:7).

Thus clouds often signify God's glory. On such occasions they indicate a theophany. And here we are told quite specifically that in disappearing into the cloud Jesus was in point of fact being taken into heaven itself: '"Men of Galilee," they said, "why do you stand here looking into the sky? This same Jesus, who has been taken from you into *heaven*, will come back in the same way you have seen him go into *heaven*"' (Acts 1:11, emphasis added). We are not to think that Jesus went up into the cloud and kept on going like a rocket. No, he was being received into the glory-cloud. It was a visible expression that Jesus was being glorified, as he had prayed in the upper room. God the Father was taking his Son and saying in visible form, 'Welcome home, my beloved Son. Welcome home!' The cloud was, in Chrysostom's words 'the royal chariot ... sent for him'.[2] Interestingly, the very same word is used in the Acts account of Jesus' ascent into the cloud (*analambanesthai*, 'taken up', Acts 1:2,11,22) as was used in the Greek translation of the Old Testament (the so-called Septuagint) account of the ascension of Elijah in a chariot (2 Kings 2:11).

In the so-called high-priestly prayer, Jesus had asked his Father, 'Father, glorify me in your presence with the glory I had with you before the world began' (John 17:5). Jesus specified two reasons for his glorification: first, 'Glorify your Son, that your Son may glorify you'; and second, 'that he might give eternal life to all those you have given him' (John 17:1,2). The Saviour applies the work of redemption only as a consequence of his exaltation, his glorification. The glory which had been hidden during his incarnate life (and briefly glimpsed on the Mount of Transfiguration — Matt. 17:2; Mark 9:2; cf. John 1:14, 'We have seen his glory') was now, in the cloud, and out of view of the disciples, restored in all its fulness.

Throughout his incarnate life on earth, Jesus' glory was veiled. He was in 'the very nature of a servant, being made in human likeness ... and ... in appearance as a man' (Phil. 2:7-8). When men looked at Jesus, all they saw was a man. He was perfectly ordinary. There were no haloes, no marks of his royal identity. To the human eye, only the marks of poverty, frailty and rejection were visible. The disciples further witnessed his crucifixion and burial — to all intents and purposes he was a blasphemer, a failure, on the verge of eternal ruin, who had been heard to cry, 'My God, my God, why have you forsaken me?' (Matt. 27:46). But now, in his resurrection, and even more so in his ascension, the veil, which had been entirely effective, was removed. He was 'taken up in glory' (1 Tim. 3:16).

The cloud served two purposes:

1. As a visible expression of Jesus' ascent into heaven

Where is heaven? The answer is something we shall have to consider in some detail, but for now it is sufficient to recall that for most people, it is 'up there'! What better way to picture it than for Jesus to slip into a cloud in the sky? Jesus' rising wasn't a lesson in spatial trajectory. The disciples were being taught a visible lesson about heaven. Jesus' disappearance was, said C. S. Lewis, a bit like an actor on stage who slips out of sight between two curtains, but appears as though he slips into one of its many folds. So Jesus disappears into a 'fold' in space.[3] He had gone to prepare a *place* for his own people to join him.

There is no need for us to doubt the literal nature of Jesus' ascension, so long as we keep in mind its purpose. It would have been perfectly possible for him to have gone to his Father in some other way, by simply disappearing, for example (something which had happened on many occasions in between successive resurrection appearances). The reason he ascended before the eyes of the disciples was to underline its *finality.* He had disappeared before, only to return again. This time he would not return — not until his triumphant appearance at the end of the age. The disciples were now able to return to Jerusalem and wait, not for Jesus to make another resurrection appearance, but for the Holy Spirit to come as he had promised.

2. *To underline his divine and stately nature*

He went up, promoted we might say. And promotion it was! His entry and exit into the world had been miraculous, an expression of divine power put forth. But whereas his entrance had been lowly and humbling, his exit was triumphant and exalting. The Man of sorrows was truly the King of kings. The disciples must now get used to fellowship without the bodily presence of Jesus, fellowship, that is, with the exalted, glorified Lord. Nowhere is this evidenced more clearly than in Jesus' words to Mary Magdalene: 'Do not hold on to me, for I have not yet returned to the Father. Go instead to my brothers and tell them, "I am returning to my Father and your Father, to my God and your God"' (John 20:17). In the ascension, Jesus was 'parted from them' (Luke 24:51, NKJV). He could no longer be seen. 'A cloud hid him from their sight' (Acts 1:9). Up till now, they had enjoyed his physical presence. They touched him, ate with him, heard his words and looked upon his face. But this relationship was now to change. Jesus had warned them that the day would come when they would no longer be able to see him (John 16:10). The bridegroom was to be taken away (Matt. 9:15) — taken away, that is, to glory! The cloud served to remind the disciples that 'Our mind is not able to ascend so high as to take a full view of the glory of Christ.'[4] Calvin is shrewd here. 'Let this cloud be a means to restrain our boldness,' he adds. There is an aspect of the majesty of God which instructs the pious to be filled with awe.

There would be a temporary sorrow at his physical departure, but their sorrow would be turned into joy (John 16:20). Calvin has written again, '[The disciples] were then taught by a surer experience that the authority he wielded and the power he exercised were sufficient for believers not only to live blessedly but also to die happily. Indeed, we see how much more abundantly he then poured out his Spirit, how much more wonderfully he advanced his kingdom, how much greater power he displayed both in helping his people and in scattering his enemies. Carried up into heaven, therefore, he withdrew his bodily presence from our sight (Acts 1:9), not to cease to be present with believers still on their earthly pilgrimage, but to rule heaven and earth with a more immediate power.'[5] Christ's departure was of a greater benefit even than his physical presence could be. As the *Heidelberg Catechism* expresses it, he is in heaven 'for our interest' (Question 46). What this 'interest' is, we shall see in the following chapters, but one thing is certain: his exit bore all the hallmarks of miracle and splendour. It was redolent of God's power (and Christ's power!). By power he disappeared into the other side of reality, to the world we call heaven. And from there he will return again. Power is now what awaited the disciples — Holy Spirit power!

It would be a mistake, however, to think of the ascension merely in terms of what it meant for the disciples. That is a part of its significance, but only a part. Another feature of the ascension lay in its significance for Jesus himself. He endured the cross, the letter to the Hebrews tells us, 'for the joy set before him' (Heb. 12:2). The four great events in Jesus' life are spoken of in the Bible both actively and passively, as deeds done both *by* Jesus and *to* Jesus. With respect to his birth, we are told that he both came and was sent; as for his death, he both gave himself and was offered; as for the resurrection, he both rose and was raised; and with respect to the ascension, he both ascended and was exalted. In the case of his birth and death, the active is more common: the emphasis is upon Jesus' own deliberate choice in coming and dying. In the case of the resurrection and the ascension, however, the passive is more common. He was raised from the tomb and exalted to the throne of heaven. It was the Father's act in calling home one whom he loved with all of his heart. It was now time for the greatest reunion that has ever been. Jesus depicted the returning prodigal son being embraced by his father and welcomed with an extravagant party. No one can imagine the joy when Jesus returned home. No words can adequately express the jubilation. It is greater than we can conceive. What joy there must have been!

2.

'Coming home': Jesus presenting himself before his Father in heaven

When Jesus disappeared through the cloud out of sight of the disciples below, where did he go? In the epistle to the Hebrews we read that he 'entered heaven itself, now to appear for us in God's presence' (Heb. 9:24). He was coming home to meet his Father.

Christ's ascension to his Father's presence was part II of a two-part event (the resurrection being part I). John Calvin is credited with describing the work of Christ in terms of the three offices of Prophet, Priest and King.[1] In ascending to his Father's throne in heaven, Jesus revealed himself as King over all the forces of darkness which attempted, but failed, to keep him down here on earth. In ascending the way he did, through a glory-cloud, he was fulfilling his prophetic role, teaching those who witnessed it that there was more to Jesus than met the eye. Glory was what the cloud signalled, and glory was where Jesus belonged.

But by far and away the most important aspect of what the ascension is about lies in the domain of Christ's role as Priest. John Murray has written, 'The heavenly high priesthood of Christ means, therefore, that Christ appears in the presence of God at the right hand of the throne of the majesty in the heavens to present himself as the perfected high priest to plead on the basis of what he has accomplished the fulfilment of all the promises, the bestowment of all the benefits, and enduement with all the graces secured and ratified by his own high priestly offering.'[2]

After Jesus ascended, he presented himself before his Father. His return was more than a home-coming; it was a demonstration that he had fulfilled every requirement of the covenant as regards the work of redemption. The Servant of the Lord had both suffered the penalty of the broken law on our behalf and at the same time obeyed its every precept.[3] Everything necessary for the salvation of sinners had been achieved. That aspect of the work, at least, was finished, never to be taken up again.

Heaven pictured in the tabernacle

Hebrews 9 is the culmination of an argument that has been developing in Hebrews as far back as the seventh chapter. At the risk of over-simplification, the writer is developing the argument that, living as they do in the days of fulfilment, these Hebrew Christians are better off on two counts: they have a better covenant, founded on, and accompanied by, better promises. Part of his argument is to point to where Christ is now (heaven) and signal that whatever was accomplished under the Old Covenant administration, with its tabernacle (and later temple) ceremonies, its provisions were both inadequate and provisional since everything took place in an 'earthly sanctuary' (Heb. 9:1).

Having mentioned the 'earthly sanctuary', the writer continues with what at first appears to be a detailed description of the tabernacle, including its general layout and furniture:

A tabernacle was set up. In its first room were the lampstand, the table and the consecrated bread; this was called the Holy Place. Behind the second curtain was a room called the Most Holy Place, which had the golden altar of incense and the gold-covered ark of the covenant. This ark contained the gold jar of manna, Aaron's staff that had budded, and the stone tablets of the covenant. Above the ark were the cherubim of the Glory, overshadowing the atonement cover. But we cannot discuss these things in detail now.

When everything had been arranged like this, the priests entered regularly into the outer room to carry on their ministry. But only the high priest entered the inner room, and that only once a year, and never without blood, which he offered for himself and for the sins the people had committed in ignorance. The Holy Spirit was showing by this that the way into the Most Holy Place had not yet been disclosed as long as the first tabernacle was still standing. This is an illustration for the present time, indicating that the gifts and sacrifices being offered were not able to clear the conscience of the worshipper. They are only a matter of food and drink and various ceremonial washings — external regulations applying until the time of the new order (Heb. 9:2-10).

Everything about the tabernacle was meant to be a 'copy' (Heb. 9:24) or 'shadow of what is in heaven' (Heb. 8:5). The very architectural layout of the tabernacle was in some way replicating heaven itself. It showed what God was like. It also showed how sinners can (and cannot) approach him. It symbolized the need for a Mediator, and what that Mediator would need to do in order to atone for sin.

The design and contents of the tabernacle

The tabernacle itself consisted of an outer curtain, to all intents and purposes a fence, which measured fifty cubits by a

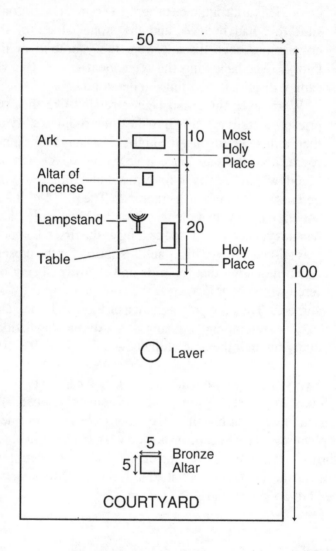

The design of the tabernacle

hundred cubits (Exod. 27:9-19). Inside was a courtyard, where worshippers would come, some on a daily basis, to offer sacrifices on the altar of burnt offering which stood at the centre. Then came the 'laver', a bronze basin containing water and used for 'ceremonial washings' (Heb. 9:10, 'baptisms' in the Greek). Further within the tabernacle was another curtain, measuring ten cubits by thirty cubits, dividing off the outer courtyard from the two inner rooms of the Holy Place, measuring ten by twenty cubits, and behind it yet another curtain, the Most Holy Place (or, the Holy of Holies), itself measuring a perfect square — ten by ten cubits.

More furniture was to be found in both of the inner rooms of the tabernacle. Within the Holy Place were three objects. In the middle of the Holy Place were a lampstand on one side (Exod. 27:20-21; Lev. 24:1-4) and, adjacent to it, a table with bread on it (Exod. 25:23-30). At the far end, and adjacent to another curtain, was an altar upon which the fumes of burning incense rose continually. Beyond the curtain was a room containing the ark of the covenant, a box covered in gold. It had a special cover, or lid, known as the 'mercy seat' or 'atonement cover'. Inside it were the tablets of stone containing the handwritten signature of God's law, and (for a while at least) the gold jar of manna and Aaron's special staff. At either end of the 'mercy seat', with wings outstretched to touch each other, were two golden cherubim.

Provisional and inadequate

Each piece of furniture was highly symbolic, a 'shadow' of another and greater reality in heaven, but to elaborate on them in this way would not have served the writer's purpose: 'But we cannot discuss these things in detail now' (Heb. 9:5). His point is to draw attention to the fact that access into the Holy of Holies, where God's *shekinah* presence was to be found, was only available to the high priest (not even the priests could enter here); and that the high priest could only enter once a year, on the Day of Atonement (Heb. 9:7), thus signalling the *provisional* nature of the Old Covenant. In addition, the sacrifices offered for atonement, namely those of animals, were offered continually, thereby signalling the *inadequacy* of these sacrifices. The Holy Spirit was showing by means of these two facts 'that the way into the Most Holy Place had not yet been disclosed' (Heb. 9:8).

In the layout of the tabernacle, the courtyard represented earth and the Holy of Holies represented God's presence (heaven). Whenever the high priest entered the Most Holy Place, he was symbolically entering heaven. In reality, he was not, of course. As Stephen was to point out, to his cost, God does not dwell in a man-made temple (or tabernacle, cf. Acts 7:48-50). Jesus, on the other hand, in pursuance of his priestly office, 'entered the Most Holy Place' (Heb. 9:12). He entered 'heaven itself' (Heb. 9:24). He passed 'through the heavens' (Heb. 4:14), through a fold in space as C. S. Lewis thought of it, and into the presence of his Father.

And this increases faith: 'We have this hope as an anchor for the soul, firm and secure. It enters the inner sanctuary behind the curtain, where Jesus, who went before us, has entered on our behalf' (Heb. 6:20). That we have a High Priest *in heaven itself* who engages in his priestly work on our behalf is what fires us with boldness. Miserable sinners though we are, we are represented in heaven, and one day will be present there, in God's presence — ransomed, healed, restored and forgiven! 'Therefore, brothers, since we have confidence to enter the Most Holy Place by the blood of Jesus, by a new and living way opened for us through the curtain, that is, his body, and since we have a great priest over the house of God, let us draw near to God with a sincere heart in full assurance of faith, having our hearts sprinkled to cleanse us from a guilty conscience and having our bodies washed with pure water' (Heb. 10:19-22).

Heaven! Yes, heaven itself is where he went, and probably this was not the first time he had appeared there since his resurrection. Heaven was his home, and since both in Hebrew and Greek the word means 'sky', it seems appropriate that in entering it, Jesus should have physically risen into the sky and disappeared into a cloud. To be in heaven and to be in God's presence is one and the same thing: heaven is God's home (Ps. 33:13-14; Matt. 6:9). It is one of the promises that shine brightly in the Scriptures that one day Christ's people will be with their Saviour for ever (John 17:5,24; 1 Thess. 4:16-17). To gain it for us, Christ now enters heaven and presents himself to his Father. It is time to ask in what capacity does he present himself? The answer to this question seems to lie along three lines.

1. Mediator of the new covenant

Firstly, Christ presents himself as the mediator of the new covenant. In order to accomplish our redemption, God pledged himself in covenant. It is a key idea (and some think it *the* key idea) of what the Bible has to say. God makes and keeps covenant. The Bible is the book of his covenant.

What is a covenant?

The word (*berith* in the Old Testament, *diatheke* in the New Testament) has the meaning of a bond. At the heart of God's covenant with man is the promise: 'I will be your God, and you shall be my people.' By covenant, persons become committed to each other, and in the case of God's covenant, this commitment is formalized and confirmed by a solemn oath of loyalty, involving an expression of self-cursing should God ever fail to comply with the terms of the covenant. Thus, when God made a covenant with Abraham, he staked his own existence on keeping it! (Heb. 6:13-18). Covenants are often accompanied by signs, visual tokens that remind the parties involved of the binding nature of the covenant and the oath which confirmed it. At different times in the history of redemption, the Sabbath, the rainbow, circumcision and baptism have served as signs.

The shedding of blood

How can God ever enter into a covenant with man, a sinner? Is it possible for God to retain his integrity and still enter into a commitment of fellowship with those who transgress the law? Biblical covenants involving the redemption of sinners have always taken this into account by insisting that such covenants require a ritual of blood-shedding to validate them. That is what the writer to the Hebrews is referring to when he says, 'This is why even the first covenant was not put into effect without blood' (Heb. 9:18), and 'In fact, the law requires that nearly everything be cleansed with blood, and without the shedding of blood there is no forgiveness' (Heb. 9:22).

Indeed, Hebrews 9 describes the ritual involved in the covenant made with Moses: 'When Moses had proclaimed every commandment of the law to all the people, he took the blood of calves, together with water, scarlet wool and branches of hyssop, and sprinkled the scroll and all the people. He said, "This is the blood of the covenant, which God has commanded you to keep"' (Heb. 9:19-21).

'Blood' and 'covenant' in these verses remind us of the ceremony at Sinai when God made a covenant with Moses

(Exod. 24:4-8). A similar ritual had taken place when God made a covenant with Abraham: a flaming torch (symbolic of God's presence) passed between the severed pieces of slain sacrificial animals (Gen. 15:17). And the connection between the two events is more than a passing one: for the covenant with Moses was an elaboration of the covenant with Abraham: 'He remembered his covenant with Abraham, with Isaac and with Jacob. So God looked on the Israelites and was concerned about them' (Exod. 2:24-25). He revealed himself to Moses as the covenant God of Abraham, Isaac and Jacob (Exod. 3:6). Moses was being informed *how* the promise to his forefathers was going to be kept.

In the Old Testament, there existed an understanding that blood-shedding was a necessary part of covenant ratification. The covenant-maker was either sprinkled with blood or he passed between the divided carcasses of slain animals (Exod. 24:7-8; cf. Jer. 34:18-19). Something very symbolic was being portrayed by this ritual: the death of the covenant-maker. It was as though the one making the covenant was saying, 'The Lord do so to me, and more also if...' (cf. Ruth 1:17; 1 Sam. 3:17, NKJV).

Covenant or testament?

Despite the fact that the same Greek word is used throughout this chapter, Bible translators have nearly always translated the word in Hebrews 9:16-17 as 'testament' rather than 'covenant'.[4] This is probably a mistake, due to a failure to appreciate that covenants *also* required this symbolic death ritual in order to make them valid.[5]

Jesus is the mediator of the new covenant (Heb. 9:15; cf. 7:22; 8:6). His death was covenantal.[6] Covenants involve curses as well as blessings (Deut. 28). The Israelites had failed to continue in the covenant and could only expect its curses. The new covenant, inaugurated by Christ's own shed blood ('This is my blood of the new covenant', Matt. 26:28), was a signal that the curses deserved were met by God's own Son as he bore the penalty of the broken covenant in his own body. His death served both the inauguration of the covenant, making good God's promise, and the substitutionary infliction of its penalty, not upon those who deserved it, but upon himself.

All of this was portrayed in a strange ritual enacted by God's people when they entered Canaan. In view of Elon Moreh, the mountain on which Abraham had first glimpsed the promised land, half the tribes stood on Mount Ebal below, and the other half on Mount Gerizim adjacent to it. As Moses read the law, in response to blessings and the curses the people were to say 'Amen'. This ritual was a covenant renewal ceremony in which the people were formally binding themselves to the covenant, its blessings and curses (Josh. 8:30-35). Curses were what they deserved, and had the old covenant had its way, curses are what all mankind would have received. It is part of the glory of the new covenant ministry of Jesus Christ that he takes the place of sinners, and in so doing binds himself to the terms of that covenant. That is the reason why he died. He died a covenantally cursed death. The anathema of the covenant came down upon him. He bore the penalty that sin deserved. He was not merely the victim of the anger and hatred of men; he was put to death by God himself. The Father 'gave up' his Son for us in order that we might not be given up, but received into God's presence (Rom. 8:32). In this way, Christ becomes the 'Amen'. In the words of Sinclair Ferguson: 'He is the One who has perfectly said "Amen" to God's law by obeying it. But he is also the One who has said "Amen" to the curse and judgement of God by standing in the place of his people, on Mount Golgotha, and accepting the wrath of God against our sin. He seals the covenant with his own blood. That is what it cost him to become the "Amen" of God (2 Cor. 1:20; Rev. 3:14).'[7]

We have been asking the question: in what capacity did Jesus present himself before his Father in heaven? In the first place, we have seen that he presents himself as the mediator of the new covenant. We now look at another aspect.

2. The perfect High Priest

Secondly, Christ presented himself as a perfect High Priest. Jesus' covenantal death secured something which Old Testament (Levitical) priests could not. Whereas the old covenant was both inadequate and provisional, Christ's death as the mediator of the new covenant was adequate and permanent. It was adequate to provide redemption for all who were liable to the curse for transgressions under the first covenant (Heb. 9:15). But the death of Jesus did something else: it cleansed the conscience and liberated sinners to serve God (Heb. 9:14).

Christ's death provides a permanent solution to the broken covenant. He died 'once for all' (Heb. 9:12). The Levitical priests made regular entries into the Holy Place (Heb. 9:6), and the high priests made annual entries into the Holy of Holies (Heb. 9:7); but Christ did not 'enter heaven to offer himself again and again' (Heb. 9:25). He has 'appeared once for all at the end of the ages to do away with sin by the sacrifice of himself' (Heb. 9:26).

What does Jesus present before his Father?

'It is finished,' Jesus uttered on the cross (John 19:30). The work necessary to accomplish redemption has been done: 'I have brought you glory on earth by completing the work you gave me to do,' Jesus said (John 17:4). But what exactly does Jesus present to the Father when he appears before his throne? Certain commentators in the past spoke of Christ actually taking his blood with him to 'offer' before his Father. Some even went as far as to suggest that in the crucifixion Christ was drained of all his blood, thus explaining why, in John's vision in Revelation 1:14, his head (face) was white! This view requires that the risen, ascended body of Jesus be bloodless, and confirmation of it has been sought in certain translations of Hebrews 9:12![8] But such a view is misguided.[9]

Associated with the idea of Christ's blood being eternally separated from his body is the notion that in some way it is being perpetually offered before the throne. Eucharistic interpreters have often cited the mass as an earthly representation of what is taking place in heaven: the perpetual offering of the blood of Christ. But the writer insists on the 'once for all' aspect of Christ's offering. Seven times he repeats it: Christ died once (Heb. 9:12,25,26,28; 10:10,12,14). As Philip Hughes remarks, 'It is the *efficacy* of the one offering made at Calvary, not the offering itself, which is perpetual.'[10] Christ offers his finished work before his Father's throne.

What else does Jesus present before his Father?

3. Christ presents himself in heaven for us

Jesus' death was not for himself, but *for us*. 'For Christ ... entered heaven itself, now to appear *for us* in God's presence' (Heb. 9:24, emphasis added). He was made sin for us. He suffered for us. He bore the curse for us. He died for us.

He was pierced for our transgressions,
    he was crushed for our iniquities;

the punishment that brought us peace was upon him,
    and by his wounds we are healed.
We all, like sheep, have gone astray,
    each of us has turned to his own way;
and the LORD has laid on him
    the iniquity of us all

                    (Isa. 53:5-6).

In the language of the Reformers, he made 'the great exchange'. He took what was ours in order that we might receive what was his. He took the curses in order that the blessings might be credited to our account. He cried out, 'My God, my God, why have you forsaken me?' in order that we might never be forsaken by God.

Do we really appreciate what it is that Jesus has done for us? And not only that, have we appreciated the love of the Father in handing over his Son to redeem us in this way? Have we, not only an inadequate view of Jesus, but an equally inadequate view of God the Father? Many Christians are paralysed because they have failed to appreciate that the entire Trinity is at work in our salvation. When Christ appeared before his Father as our representative, the Father's heart must have been near to bursting asunder with satisfaction. We can almost hear him saying in the hearing of all of heaven: 'This is my Son!' Never had the Father loved his Son more than in the hours when he hung on the cross. 'The reason my Father loves me is that I lay down my life,' Jesus had said (John 10:17). And now that death is passed, the agony behind him, and Jesus enters into his glory to claim his reward, the Father is ready to give him all he asks.

Jesus has come home. He is where he belongs. He is in the company of those whom he loves.

Hark, those bursts of acclamation!
Hark, those loud triumphant chords!
Jesus takes the highest station:
Oh, what joy the sight affords!
Crown him! Crown him!
King of kings, and Lord of lords!

                              Thomas Kelly (1769-1855)[11]

3.
Jesus receives a crown

The writings of C. S. Lewis have always been popular. Perhaps none are so immediately appealing as his set of children's tales *The Chronicles of Narnia*, where a group of children pass through the back of a wardrobe and emerge in another world, the land of Narnia. In the final volume of the series, *The Last Battle*, they pass through what appears to be a stable door and find themselves in a world full of beauty. One of the young people is heard to say, 'In our world too, a stable once had something inside it that was bigger than our whole world.'[1]

There was always something 'bigger' about Jesus than the human eye could see or the human mind appreciate. Throughout his earthly ministry, Jesus was conscious of a glory that belonged to him as of right, a glory which had been veiled by the incarnation, but restored to him upon his departure from this world. Here we find the explanation for that prayer he uttered in the upper room: 'Father, the time has come. Glorify your Son, that your Son may glorify you... And now, Father, glorify me in your presence with the glory I had with you before the world began' (John 17:1,5). In this prayer, Jesus reveals a consciousness of both a pre-existent and an exalted state, an existence before and after his present state of humiliation and suffering.

In considering the ascension of Jesus we have noted that in going up into the cloud and disappearing, he left the disciples staring into the sky. He had gone up, a movement which was itself highly symbolic. God the Father was not only removing his Son from the world — removing him to a condition of perfect blessedness, away from harassment, pain, suffering and death; he was also drawing his Son closer to himself. In effect Jesus was promoted: he had quite literally 'gone up in the world'. To cite J. I. Packer, 'The Son was now recalled to headquarters to become managing director.'[2]

How is this promotion to be evaluated? Paul expressed it in this way: 'Therefore God also has highly exalted him...' (Phil. 2:9, NKJV). In fact Philippians 2:5-11 recounts how this exaltation is to be conceived.

> ... Christ Jesus:
> Who, being in very nature God,
>   did not consider equality with God something to be
>   grasped,
> but made himself nothing,
>   taking the very nature of a servant,
>   being made in human likeness.
> And being found in appearance as a man,
>   he humbled himself
>   and became obedient to death — even death on a
>   cross!
> Therefore God exalted him to the highest place
>   and gave him the name that is above every name,
> that at the name of Jesus every knee should bow,
>   in heaven and on earth and under the earth,
> and every tongue confess that Jesus Christ is Lord,
>   to the glory of God the Father.

We are told that there are two things to be noted about Jesus' incarnate ministry: first, he took the form of 'a servant', and second, he was in likeness as a man (v. 7).

A servant

The word 'form' *(morphe)* had all kinds of classical associations in Paul's day, and his use of this precise word no doubt reflects some of these origins. In classical usage, *morphe* meant something akin to 'essence'. Those essential qualities and characteristics that make something what it is are its *morphe*, its form. Whatever constitutes a servant, Jesus assumed it. He actually became a servant. It was not a pretence; it was as real and genuine as it is possible to be. But what does being a servant involve? Essentially, it means being under authority, being totally subject to the law. Jesus was *obedient* in every way.[3]

No passage of Scripture is more important in capturing this aspect of the Saviour's work than the fourth Servant Song in Isaiah 52:13 - 53:12: 'See, my servant...' (Isa. 52:13; cf. 42:1). 'By his knowledge my righteous servant will justify many, and he will bear their iniquities' (Isa. 53:11). The Messiah is God's servant, not man's. His obedience is rendered to God. He comes to fulfil everything demanded of him by God.

Think of the words of Jesus at the outset of his public ministry. John protested at the thought of Jesus' being baptized, identifying in such an act with the need for forgiveness and cleansing. 'Let it be so now,' Jesus was heard to say, 'it is proper for us to do this to fulfil all righteousness' (Matt. 3:15). Think, too, of other statements which Jesus uttered: 'My food ... is to do the will of him who sent me and to finish his work' (John 4:34). 'For I have come down from heaven not to do my will but to do the will of him who sent me' (John 6:38). 'The reason my Father loves me is that I lay down my life — only to take it up again. No one takes it from me, but I lay it down of my own accord. I have authority to lay it down and authority to take it up again. This command I received from my Father' (John 10:17-18). Christ's obedience was total and unremitting. He 'became obedient to death' (Phil. 2:8).

In agreeing to become the mediator of the covenant, Jesus was placed under obligation to fulfil the law's requirements. This was his achievement as he drew near to Calvary: 'I have brought you glory on earth by completing the work you gave me to do' (John 17:4). No matter how difficult it became, Jesus never flinched from what was expected of him. Think of his life: born in a stable, miles away from home; exiled into Egypt; raised in Nazareth — a town about which folk said, 'Nazareth! Can anything good come from there?' (John 1:46). Then there was the poverty of his existence, the constant rejection of his ministry, the denial by a close friend, the betrayal by one of his own disciples. He was beaten, spat upon and ultimately crucified as a common criminal. And, all his life, Jesus never flinched from his obedience. He was utterly submissive.

A man

Not only was Jesus in the form of a servant; he was also a man (Phil. 2:7). Paul uses two expressions to underline the humanness of Jesus. He was in 'human likeness' (v. 7) and 'in appearance as a man' (v. 8). There is no essential difference in the meaning between 'form' and 'likeness'. Just as Jesus was essentially a servant, assuming all the characteristics of a servant; so he assumed all the essential properties and distinctions of a human being, a man. What does this mean exactly? It means that Jesus was in possession of a real human body. It was made up of flesh and blood and bones. Its physiology, its anatomical nature, its genetic constitution, its chemistry — everything about it was human. There was nothing to distinguish the body of Jesus from any other human body. He 'became flesh and made his dwelling among us' (John 1:14). He was subject to all the limitations of a human body: he became hungry and thirsty; he grew tired and required sleep; he experienced the intensity and hurt of pain and discomfort; he could actually die.

That Jesus was a real man means he was a 'reasonable soul'.⁴ It is important to stress this point, due to an error that developed in the early church, propagated by a man named Apollinarius, in which he asserted that in order to preserve the deity of Christ we must guard against saying that Jesus was in possession of a human soul. But the church was right to condemn this teaching as a heresy. If Jesus was fully human, he must necessarily have had a human soul, a human psychology. He had a human mind and human emotions and human affections and a human will. There is all the emphasis upon what our Lord felt, and feared; what our Lord was ignorant of and what he wrestled against.

Having emphasized his obedience, we must not think that because he was divine he rendered that obedience easily, without any struggle. The Garden of Gethsemane witnessed a titanic conflict of will, one in which every ounce of our Saviour's humanness recoiled against the thought of crucifixion. He would not have been human, nor could he have sympathized with our revulsion to it, had he himself not experienced the battle of wills: the will of his own humanity and the will of his Father in heaven. As Calvin put it, 'It follows then that His human soul had different desires from the hidden purpose of God.'⁵ It is the supreme expression of his complete submission to his Father in heaven that Jesus was heard to say, 'Not my will, but yours be done' (Luke 22:42).

What did Jesus look like?

There is one more feature which Paul highlights. He was 'in appearance as a man' (Phil. 2:8). Essentially, this is just another way of saying that he was in 'human likeness' (v. 7). But the change in language is meant to convey to us something additional. It is the appearance of Jesus, what he actually looked like to others, that is in view rather than his essential nature.

Did you ever wonder what Jesus looked like? What was the colour of his hair? What about his height, or weight? What were his distinguishing features? Did he really have a beard, as so many portraits of him assume that he had? The Gospels give us none of this information. In that respect they are quite unlike any biography that we are accustomed to. Their motivation is completely different from that of normal biographers. But these are not illicit questions to ask. No doubt we have been prevented from knowing the answers to them lest the church be forever taken up with making models (images) of Christ. But the question is still valid. What did Jesus look like? And the answer given is that in appearance he was very ordinary indeed. He did not stand apart from the crowd. He was just a man — no haloes, no giant torso, no angelic properties; nothing but ordinariness. Even though he was God and remained so during the incarnation, what men and women saw when they looked at Jesus was someone whom they regarded as a reject of society, a frail, weak, unpopular man. And there came a moment, at the cross, when all that they saw was a man 'stricken by God, smitten by him, and afflicted' (Isa. 53:4).

> Christ, by highest heaven adored,
> Christ, the everlasting Lord,
> Late in time behold him come,
> Offspring of the virgin's womb.

Veiled in flesh the Godhead see,
Hail the incarnate Deity!
Pleased as man with men to dwell,
Jesus our Emmanuel.

Charles Wesley[6]

Do you see what is being said here? Looking at Jesus, looking especially at the crucifixion, no one would have come to the conclusion that here was the Lord of glory! You might have looked up to the heavens and said, 'The heavens declare the glory of God' (Ps. 19:1). But you would not have looked at Calvary and come to the conclusion: 'This is God's Son whom he loves so much.' He appeared as one condemned and forsaken and despised and rejected. That is why Paul chooses a word which at first sounds as though it cannot be true: he 'emptied' himself (v. 7), he 'humbled' himself (v. 8). And the emptying and humbling go on and on until he dies. It begins at Bethlehem, but it progresses further and further into God-forsakenness, 'even death on a cross'. It is not enough that he should experience the obscenity of death; he must experience a crucifixion, with all its symbolism of a cursed and condemned man. This is the ultimate form of rejection! When Jesus explained to his disciples the significance of what would happen to him, he quoted from God's words in Zechariah:

Awake, O sword, against my shepherd,
    against the man who is close to me! ...
Strike the shepherd,
    and the sheep will be scattered...

(Zech. 13:7).

It was the Lord's will to crush him
    and cause him to suffer

(Isa. 53:10).

God was handing Jesus over! In Paul's language, Christ came under the curse of God (Gal. 3:13); he was made sin (2 Cor. 5:21); God did not spare him (Rom. 8:32).

In addition to what was true of Jesus during his days on earth, Paul asserts some truths relating to his existence before he came — his pre-existence. Paul is anxious for us to know something about Jesus that was true of him before he came into this world and which was also true of him after he ascended to his Father's side. What was that? It was that Jesus existed before, and continues now to exist, in a state that is both divine and glorious! Before his death, Jesus had prayed: 'And now, Father, glorify me in your presence with the glory I had with you before the world began' (John 17:5).

Here, in Philippians 2, Paul is saying the same thing. The first thing he says about Christ is this: 'Who, being in very nature God' (v. 6). Paul is thinking of the time when Jesus became incarnate and at that time Jesus *was already* in the form of God. It is exactly the same as the opening of John's Gospel: 'In the beginning *was* the Word...' (emphasis added). John is deliberately reminding us of the opening sentence of the Bible in the book of Genesis: 'In the beginning God...' (Gen. 1:1). But John is also establishing a contrast with Genesis. The first chapter of Genesis focuses on the point of creation, the very beginning of time. But John wants us to think of what was true *before* that. In the beginning, at the first moment of time itself, the Word already was! He already had an existence! The Word had a pre-existence. That is what is meant by, 'who being in the form of God...'

Pre-existent and divine

In addition, Paul is asserting the *divine nature* of his pre-existence. He was in the form of God. We have already seen what this word 'form' *(morphe)* means. From classical Greek it means those essential qualities and characteristics that make something what it is. In that case, Jesus possessed every attribute and characteristic of deity in his pre-existent state. No assertion of Christ's deity could be stronger than that. However, recent study into the meaning of New Testament words such as the word *morphe* has tended to emphasize another source of meaning, one that reflects more its usage in the Old Testament rather than in classical Greek philosophy. In the Greek translation of the Hebrew Old Testament Scriptures, an important fact emerges: the word *morphe* is used synonymously with the words 'image,' 'likeness' and 'glory'. In looking at the meaning of the word this way, we see that Jesus, in his pre-existent state, was 'the glory of God'. God's glory is what God is in very essence. God's glory in the Old Testament carries associations of his weight, worth, wealth, splendour and dignity. God was answering Moses' plea to be shown his glory when he proclaimed to Moses his name (i.e., his nature, character and power, Exod. 33:18 - 34:7). With that proclamation went an awe-inspiring physical manifestation, the *shekinah*, a bright cloud that could look like fire, white hot (Exod. 24:17). The *shekinah* was itself called the glory of God; it appeared at significant moments in the Bible story as a sign of God's active presence (Exod. 33:22; 34:5; cf. 16:7,10; 24:15-17; 40:34-38; Lev. 9:23-24; 1 Kings 8:10-11; Ezek. 1:28; 8:4; 9:3; 10:4; 11:22-23; 43:1-5; Matt. 17:5; Luke 2:9; cf. Acts 1:9; 1 Thess. 4:17; Rev. 1:7). And James, the Lord's brother, who had lived in the same house as Jesus, and maybe even slept in the same bed, nevertheless, refers to him as the 'Lord Jesus Christ, the Lord of glory' (James 2:1, NKJV — literally, 'the Lord Jesus Christ, the glory'). Few statements in the entire Word of God are more persuasive of Jesus' deity than that!

Claiming what was already his

Paul then adds another statement about Jesus: he 'did not consider equality with God something to be grasped' (Phil. 2:6). There have been two interpretations of these words and the difference between them is crucial. The first interpretation suggests that what is being said here is that Christ was not in possession of deity and that he did not reach and grasp it. That, of course, would deny his pre-existent deity. But we have already seen that Paul has insisted on his pre-existent deity by saying that he was already in the form of God when he decided to become incarnate and humble himself. No, that interpretation will not do.

Another interpretation tries to close the gap a little by suggesting that whilst it was true that Jesus was equal with God in most respects, there was an element of his equality that was missing, namely his lordship. This interpretation is very appealing in this sense, because it appears as though Paul goes on to say that after the ascension, Jesus was not merely exalted to his pre-existent condition; he was hyper-exalted. There was an aspect now of his deity after the ascension which was missing before — namely, his cosmic lordship.

Now this is impossible. We are told that all creation was brought into existence by Jesus Christ (Heb. 1:2). He is before all things and by him everything holds together (Col. 1:17). And you can go back to Isaiah's great vision in the temple, one which the New Testament says was a vision of Jesus Christ before his incarnation (John 12:41), and Isaiah tells us that he saw the Lord 'seated on a throne, high and exalted' (Isa. 6:1). That is about as clear a picture of what it means to be Lord as any. It is impossible to conceive of God without his lordship.

But there is one more possibility that needs to be considered: that in saying that Jesus emptied himself, Paul means that whilst Jesus was God in some way *before* the incarnation, he ceased to be God as soon as he humbled himself. His emptying of himself was an emptying of his deity. But that is impossible, too. Even if it is humanly conceivable to speak of God divesting himself of certain attributes of deity, theologically it makes no sense whatever. To do so would involve the death of God. He would cease to be God. But the whole point of the incarnation is that God the Father looks down upon Jesus and says, 'This *is* my Son.' He doesn't say, 'This used to be my Son.' As one writer has put it, 'This is a doctrine not of incarnation but of metamorphosis, of a divine being who ceased temporarily to be divine and became human.'[7]

The clue to the right interpretation is to see verse 6 as stating negatively what verses 7-8 state positively. What Paul is saying is this: even though he held equality with God as a right, he did not hold on to it, or clutch at it in a selfish way; he emptied himself, he humbled himself. In some way or other (and we are to be very careful indeed in defining this) he did not behave in a selfish way. In contrast to Adam, who grasped for equality with God and lost his life, Christ sacrificed his enjoyment of that equality with God which was his by right, thereby saving our lives. He did not say in fulfilling his mediatorial role as God's servant, 'If I go and become your servant, I want to go riding in a chariot of glory.' He did not insist on having all the comforts of his divine home to accompany his coming into the world. He fully agreed to the conditions of his mediatorial office: if he comes to save us from our sins, he must come 'in a low condition' (*Shorter Catechism,* Question 27).

Hyper-exalted

We have seen that the ascension of Christ sets him apart from his incarnate condition. Even though he bears the marks of humiliation for ever in his glorified flesh (cf. John 20:25,27), his humiliation is something that belongs to the past; it is something that used to be, but is no longer. But Jesus' ascension takes him into realms where he had never been before; not even his pre-existent condition can be compared to what is true of him now; for now, Jesus is not only exalted, he is hyper-exalted. What does this mean?

Does it mean, as might at first be suggested, that Paul is saying that Christ is exalted to a position that is higher than that which he had known before the incarnation? As far as the deity of Christ is concerned, that cannot be! He was God — not almost God or 99% God. He was in the form of God. He could not have been more divine; that would be a contradiction in terms. We must therefore reject any interpretation that suggests that there were elements of Christ's divinity that were missing (e.g. his lordship). What is in view here is the exaltation of the God-man. Christ had been at the right hand of God the Father before the incarnation. As to his divine nature, he had been at the right hand of God during his incarnation also. But never before had Jesus existed in heaven as the God-man. It is the placing of the glorified human nature in the midst of the throne of God that is in view when it says that God hyper-exalted him. This is the contrast that Paul is making between Christ's condition now and his condition before his incarnation.

The meaning of this hyper-exaltation is made clearer in the context: God highly exalted him, and certain responses are forthcoming. There are three in particular.

A supreme name

Following the ascension, Jesus is given a name which is above every other name. One possibility is that the name referred to is that of Jesus:

... the name that is above every name,
that at the name of Jesus every knee should bow,
    in heaven and on earth and under the earth
                                        (Phil. 2:10).

In this sense, the common name 'Jesus' (and it was a fairly common name) was now exalted to a position that far exceeded its lowly origins. Paul says something very similar in Ephesians 1:20-23, where Christ's exaltation is described as being seated above all powers and above 'every name that is named, not only in this age but also in that which is to come' (Eph. 1:21, NKJV). Of all the names the most precious now is the name of Jesus! 'How sweet the name of Jesus sounds, in a believer's ear...!' Whenever the name 'Jesus' now is sounded, it calls forth worship and praise.[8]

But another, and more widely accepted interpretation is that the name referred to is not 'Jesus' but 'Lord' *(kurios)*:

that at the name of Jesus every knee should bow,
    in heaven and on earth and under the earth,
and every tongue confess that Jesus Christ is Lord,
    to the glory of God the Father
                                        (Phil. 2:9-11).

In this case, the implications are truly staggering. Jesus, as the God-man in the midst of throne, is none other than the Covenant LORD of the Old Testament! One point in favour of this interpretation is the fact that Philippians 2:10 is almost a direct quotation of Isaiah 45:23, where the Covenant LORD, having declared himself to be the only God and the only Saviour, vows that he will be the object of universal worship and adoration. This is what the Jesus, the God-man, claims for himself right now — universal worship and adoration!

That he now bears the title 'Lord' is an interpretation that is itself fraught with difficulties. Was this not true during his incarnate life? Has he not always been Lord? His ascension did not confer on him the title of Lord. He was Lord all along. There never was a time when he was not Lord. He was Lord in the manger. He was Lord on the cross. He was Lord in the tomb. In what way, therefore, can his acquisition of the title 'Lord', a title which was always rightfully his, be said to be a hyper-exaltation? The answer has to do with the public recognition of his lordship.

Whilst Jesus always was Lord, and occasionally the title was used to designate him as such, these occasions were comparatively rare.[9] And, if we think of his ministry in the Old Testament, for example, he was God incognito! He appeared in theophanies — as 'the angel of the Lord', or as that mysterious figure, Melchizedek. And even during his incarnate life, time and again, he insisted on keeping his real identity hidden. On a number of occasions, after he had performed a miracle that would gain for him great public attention, he warned the persons healed to keep the matter secret and to avoid publicity (Mark 1:43-44; 3:11-12; 5:43; 7:36; 8:30; 9:9 etc.). The reason behind these instructions was the fact that current ideas about the Messiah were so seriously astray that Jesus needed to re-educate people as to his real identity and mission. All such restraints are now taken away. Now, he is *publicly* proclaimed as Lord.

Universal acknowledgement

In addition to receiving a name, Jesus receives acknowledgement — universal acknowledgement.

> At the name of Jesus every knee should bow,
>   in heaven and on earth and under the earth
> (Phil. 2:10).

This is not yet true in the terms spoken of here. Not everyone at this moment bows and acknowledges Jesus as Lord. Some have never heard of Jesus! But one day there will be no dispute: everyone will acknowledge him. John is given a glimpse of it:

> Then I heard every creature in heaven and on earth and under the earth and on the sea, and all that is in them, singing:
>
> 'To him who sits on the throne and to the Lamb
> be praise and honour and glory and power,
>   for ever and ever!'
>
> The four living creatures said, 'Amen,' and the elders fell down and worshipped
>
> (Rev. 5:13-14).

There will be universal acknowledgement, but not universal worship! Some of the acknowledgement will be involuntary! Calvin comments that the devils 'are not, and never will be, subject of their own accord and by cheerful submission; but Paul is not speaking here of voluntary obedience'.[10] Some will acknowledge the lordship of Christ to their shame. Having never bowed their knees in acknowledgement of his sovereign rule here and now, they will forced to admit their error in the world to come.

Either way, God is glorified: in the glorification and hyper-exaltation of the Son, the Father is glorified too. Jesus receives the name 'Lord', and this in turn signals the response of all creation in acknowledgement of his lordship, both of which are 'to the glory of God the Father' (Phil. 2:11). Jesus has returned home in triumph. His dominion will know no bounds. He has taken his seat on the throne as King of kings and Lord of lords.

No one found this truth more difficult to believe than Paul. That he should ever have come to pronounce 'Jesus is Lord' is among the most amazing facts of history. No one caused the church more problems than Saul of Tarsus. He almost single-handedly destroyed it in its cradle. Rigid monotheist that he was, the very sound of Christians singing and extolling Jesus as Lord filled him with rage. Yet God arrested him before he could arrest any more (this is the figure of speech he employs in giving testimony to his conversion in Philippians 3:12). It was enough to convince him that what he saw shining in the face of Jesus Christ was the very image and glory of God (2 Cor. 4:4-6). The ascension had confirmed Jesus' true identity.

4.
Pouring out the Holy Spirit

At nine o'clock in the morning, on the first Pentecost following the death of Jesus, the new covenant ministry of the Holy
Spirit began. It was attended by unusual phenomena: a tor-
nado-like sound; what looked like tongues of fire over the
heads of those present; and the gift of languages — an ability
to speak in a language unfamiliar to those who actually did the
speaking.

What was happening? Peter gives the explanation: 'Exalted
to the right hand of God, [Jesus] has received from the Father
the promised Holy Spirit and has poured out what you now see
and hear' (Acts 2:33). Just before his ascension, Jesus had told
the disciples to wait in Jerusalem 'for the gift my Father
promised, which you have heard me speak about' (Acts 1:4).
The pouring out of the Holy Spirit was the fulfilment of a
promise made *by* Jesus to the disciples in the upper room
shortly before his death, and prior to that by Old Testament
prophets predicting the coming of the new covenant age, and
before that *to* Jesus by the Father upon entering into a covenant
to become our Mediator and Redeemer.

On the night of his betrayal, Jesus talked at length to the
eleven disciples in the upper room in Jerusalem about this
promise of the Spirit. It was to be Jesus' continuing ministry
to them after his departure. They were understandably afraid,

not just for their Master, who was about to be taken and crucified, but anxious about their own welfare once he had gone. 'Do not let your hearts be troubled. Trust in God; trust also in me...' (John 14:1), he said to them. They were words of indescribable power. But what did they mean? How would the disciples ever cope without the presence of their Saviour? How could their sense of unease ever be allayed?

The Spirit of Jesus

The answer lies in the ministry of 'another Counsellor', a personal representative agent of Jesus who would be sent by the Father at his (the Son's) personal request, following his exodus from this world: 'And I will ask the Father, and he will give you another Counsellor to be with you for ever — the Spirit of truth. The world cannot accept him, because it neither sees him nor knows him. But you know him, for he lives with you and will be in you... But the Counsellor, the Holy Spirit, whom the Father will send in my name, will teach you all things and will remind you of everything I have said to you' (John 14:16-17,26). In describing the Holy Spirit as '*another* Counsellor', the word chosen for 'another' *(allos)* tends (not always, but certainly here) to mean 'another of the same sort', thereby signalling that the Holy Spirit is to take up a similar ministry to the disciples after Jesus leaves them. The Spirit is the Spirit of Jesus (cf. Acts 16:7; Rom. 8:9; Phil. 1:19).

A series of parallels underlines further the equivalence of Jesus' ministry on earth and the coming ministry of the Holy Spirit after Jesus' ascension. Both Jesus and the Spirit are described as teachers (John 14:23,26), and Counsellors (14:1,16,26,27); both are home-makers: Jesus, in heaven (14:2-3) and the Spirit in the hearts of believers on earth (14:23). Then again, there are further parallel statements:

'He lives with you and will be in you' (14:17).

'I will not leave you... I will come to you'(14:18).

'Before long, the world will not see me any more, but you will see me' (14:19).

'On that day you will realize that I am in my Father, and you are in me, and I am in you' (14:20).

'If anyone loves me, he will obey my teaching. My Father will love him, and we will come to him and make our home with him' (14:23).

'The Holy Spirit ... will remind you of everything I have said to you' (14:26).

We are meant to pick up the continuity of ministry that follows the ascension of Christ in the ongoing ministry of the Holy Spirit after Pentecost. The Spirit seems to pick up where Jesus leaves off. But there is more than continuity of ministry. There is something about the ministry of the Spirit that goes beyond anything they have known so far. This is why Jesus says to them, 'It is to your advantage that I go away' (16:7, NKJV).

How could it possibly be to their advantage? Evidently the disciples did not think so. They had known him in a way that we have not: they touched him, they could describe his features, his bearing — those aspects of his human personality that distinguished him from others. They loved to be with him, and some had given up much in order to do just that. And now he was going away! How could that be to their advantage? It is clear that the disciples did not think it in the least advantageous: they were troubled, afraid and confused about the immediate future. Thus Jesus spends a good deal of his time in the upper room convincing them that his physical departure is for their good.

Knowing the Holy Spirit

One of the ways Jesus ministers to their fear is by reminding the disciples that they already know the Holy Spirit: 'But you know him...,' Jesus insists (John 14:17). They knew his ministry, though they did not realize it. It was the Spirit who made known God's will to people in Old Testament times, sometimes by direct communication (Num. 24:2; 2 Sam. 23:2; 1 Chron. 12:18; Neh. 9:30; Job 32:8; Isa. 61:1-4; Ezek. 2:2, 11:24; 37:1; Micah 3:8; Zech. 7:12). It was the Spirit who taught the nature of faith and repentance, elucidating the way of fellowship with God (Ps. 51:10-12; Isa.11:2; 44:3; Joel 2:28). It was the Spirit who equipped men like Joseph, Moses, Gideon, Samson and David for service in the kingdom of God (Gen. 41:38; Num. 11:17; Judg. 6:34; 15:14; 1 Sam. 16:13). And when the disciples displayed skills which they employed in the service of the kingdom, it was the Spirit who gave them (cf. Exod. 31:1-11; 35:30-35). The Spirit was known to them in his actions and deeds in their lives, though they may not have appreciated his ministry. His distinct identity, as the Third Person of the Trinity, was something they, as yet, had not come to grasp. Only after Pentecost was this aspect of God's being fully revealed.

The disciples had also known the Holy Spirit in another way. They had witnessed his ministry in Jesus, to whom the Spirit had been given 'without limit' (John 3:34). 'He lives with you,' Jesus assured his disciples (John 14:17), meaning that they were witnessing something of the Spirit's presence and power in the life of Jesus. Jesus had, after all, been miraculously conceived by the Holy Spirit (Matt. 1:18,20; Luke 1:35). John the Baptist had drawn their attention to the way in which Jesus had been filled by the Spirit, a descending dove making the point clear (Matt. 3:16; Mark 1:10; Luke 3:21-22; cf. John 1:33). From then on, as had been true from the very start, Jesus performed every aspect of his ministry by the Spirit's power. Thus Jesus was 'led by the Spirit' to face the ordeal of temptation — a deliberate move on Jesus' part by which he declared war against the forces of darkness (Luke 4:1; Matt. 4:1; Mark 1:12). And thereafter he preached in the Spirit's power (Luke 4:18), exorcised demons by the Spirit (Matt. 12:28) and even faced crucifixion by offering himself to God 'through the eternal Spirit' (Heb. 9:14). 'Nothing was undertaken,' writes George Smeaton, 'but by the Spirit's direction; nothing spoken but by His guidance; nothing executed but by His power.'[1] The point needs to be stressed: Jesus did not draw on the resources of his deity in order to fulfil his messianic role as God's Servant; he drew on the supplies of the Holy Spirit given to him in full measure. 'The second person of the Godhead, humbling himself in human flesh,' writes Hugh Martin, 'did not draw directly on his own divine resources, but suffering his humanity to feel all its own insufficiency as a weak, dependent creature, he drew all his strength from God through the Spirit.'[2]

'You know him, for he lives with you,' Jesus said, meaning that what they saw every day in his life and ministry was the power of the Holy Spirit at work. And he 'will be in you', he adds. What had up till now been somewhat vague and external, would, after Pentecost, be clearer and in their hearts in a way that had not been true before. And even though their experience of the Spirit was to be new, the Spirit himself was not. What they were being promised in the upper room was a continuation of that ministry which they had already known in some measure (though they had not realized it) and, moreover, a ministry which they had seen in the life and testimony of Jesus. The Holy Spirit, when he comes, Jesus assures them, 'will testify about me' (John 15:26). The Holy Spirit's ministry is self-effacing, directing all his energies to another, that is, to Jesus Christ. As floodlights draw attention, not to themselves, but the objects upon which they shine, so the Holy Spirit never seeks to highlight himself so much as the Son, whose life and ministry he ever lives to enhance.[3]

The Spirit and the cross

All of this highlights the once-and-for-all aspect of Pentecost. The sending of the Holy Spirit is as a direct result of the ascension and in that respect it is unrepeatable. It is no more repeatable than the crucifixion, death, resurrection or ascension of Jesus Christ.

In particular, there is an intimate connection between the Spirit and the cross. What Jesus was only able to promise before his death, he actually bestowed as a result of his ascension to his Father in heaven. 'Exalted to the right hand of God, he has received from the Father the promised Holy Spirit...', Peter explained in his Pentecost sermon (Acts 2:33).

Even before the Farewell Discourse, Jesus had signalled that he would bestow the Holy Spirit upon the disciples. He did so in John 7:37-39: 'On the last and greatest day of the Feast, Jesus stood and said in a loud voice, "If anyone is thirsty, let him come to me and drink. Whoever believes in me, as the Scripture has said, streams of living water will flow from within him." By this he meant the Spirit, whom those who believed in him were later to receive. Up to that time the Spirit had not been given, since Jesus had not yet been glorified.'

One of the interesting things that occurred at the Feast of Tabernacles was that the high priest would fill a golden pitcher with water drawn from the pool of Siloam, and lead a procession back to the temple. At a certain point in the celebrations the priest would pour the water through a conduit which led to the base of the altar of burnt offering. Tabernacles was a harvest festival and associated with the need for, and provision of, rain. The water was therefore highly significant of recent provision in the harvest. But more than that, it was a reminder that God had provided water for the people of God out of a rock in Moses' time. That rock was Christ, Paul argues (1 Cor. 10:4) and it is highly significant that Jesus, at this festival, urges them to come to him for 'living water'.

The Feast of Tabernacles became associated with other passages, especially those prophetic passages which urged the people to seek salvation from those wells which have their source in God himself. 'With joy you will draw water from the wells of salvation,' Isaiah had prophesied (Isa. 12:3). Perhaps it was at the very moment when the choirs in the temple sang one of the *Hallel* psalms: 'O LORD, save us; O LORD, grant us success' (Ps. 118:25) that Jesus spoke these words. The source of salvation and the source of the Spirit is from him alone.

A problem associated with Jesus' words in John concerns the meaning of 'within him'. Streams of living water will flow from 'within him'. To whom does the 'him' refer? Does it refer to Christians, as though Jesus were saying that the Holy Spirit will flow from inside the believer (a view taken by Origen and the Eastern church in particular). Or does it refer to Jesus? In this case what is being said is that the Spirit will flow from within Jesus to the believer — a view that harmonizes with a vivid picture given in Ezekiel 47 of a river that flows from beneath the very temple out to the Dead Sea. It is thought that worshippers at the Feast of Tabernacles would have been reminded of this vision.[4] In this connection it is helpful to recall that on the cross a spear was thrust into Jesus' side, 'bringing', according to John, 'a sudden flow of blood and water' (John 19:34). The water is symbolic of cleansing (John 3:5), life (4:14) and the Spirit (7:38-39) and when, following his resurrection, Jesus encouraged Thomas to thrust his hand into his pierced side, he was surely indicating it was from this very wound that blood and water had flowed. Soon,

upon Jesus' return to the Father and his consequent glorification, the Spirit would be sent.

That is why the disciples had no need to be afraid. Even
though Jesus was going to leave them, he was going to come
to them again. Every day of their lives, the Holy Spirit, who
after Pentecost would dwell in them, would remind them of
Jesus and take them into a deeper appreciation of him than they
ever realized. As a result of Jesus' death, and only as such, a
new appreciation of their relationship to God through Jesus
Christ would dawn.

The Holy Spirit's names

As the personal representative of Jesus, the Holy Spirit is said
to continue the very ministry of Jesus. As we have already
indicated, both Jesus and the Spirit are described as teachers
(14:23,26) and Counsellors (14:1,16,26-27); and both are
home-makers — Jesus, in heaven (14:2-3) and the Spirit in the
hearts of believers on earth (14:23).

The Teacher

Jesus is our Teacher. He explained to the disciples in the upper
room that one of the hallmarks of a Christian disciple is that
'He will obey my teaching' (John 14:23). Likewise, when the
Holy Spirit comes, he 'will teach you all things' (14:26). Nor
does Jesus leave them in the dark as to the content of what the
Spirit will teach: 'On that day you will realize that I am in my
Father, and you are in me, and I am in you' (John 14:20).

The Spirit will teach them concerning Jesus' relationship to
the Father: 'I am in my Father.' There is an entire universe of
meaning in the use of the preposition 'in' at this point. It
alludes to the relationship of divine fellowship that exists

between Jesus and his Father in heaven. It refers to their union in deity and communion in mutual love. In an earlier incident with unbelieving Jews, Jesus had pleaded with them to believe that 'The Father is in me, and I in the Father' (10:38).

The Father loved the Son and the Son loved the Father. And there is something about love that makes us want to be in someone — in their thoughts and in their hearts! In the incarnate life and ministry of Jesus, in every step of the way, the Father looked down with a mixture of pride and grief as he observed the ongoing obedience of his Son. On two occasions God was heard to say, 'This is my Son' (Matt. 3:17; 17:5). Paul spoke of the ministry of the Holy Spirit as he 'searches all things, even the deep things of God' (1 Cor. 2:10). The Spirit shows us some of the deep things! And there is nothing deeper than the relationship that exists between the Father and the Son.

Then again, the Holy Spirit will teach the disciples something of the nature of their relationship with Jesus and Jesus' relationship with them. 'You are in me, and I am in you' (John 14:20). 'Union with Christ', wrote John Murray, 'is ... the central truth of the whole doctrine of salvation... It is not simply a phase of the application of redemption; it underlies every aspect of redemption...'[5] The phrases 'in Christ', 'in the Lord', or 'in him' occur 164 times in the New Testament — all of them in Paul's letters, thus testifying to the importance of this truth (1 Cor. 1:2; Eph. 1:1; Phil. 1:1; Col. 1:2, etc.). A Christian is someone who is united to Christ. Paul could say of Andronicus and Junias that they were 'in Christ' before he was, meaning that they became Christians before he did (Rom. 16:7). This has profound implications, as Saul of Tarsus was to learn, for in persecuting Christians he was to be forcibly reminded that he was in effect persecuting Christ: 'Saul, Saul, why do you persecute me?' (Acts 9:4). The importance of the truth is best captured in something that Paul wrote: 'I consider

everything a loss ... that I may gain Christ and be found in him'
(Phil. 3:8-9). The Spirit had taught him the relevance of his
union with Jesus Christ.

This helps us appreciate *who we are*. As Christians we are
radically different from what we were as unbelievers. Regen-
eration has transformed us entirely. Our union with Christ has
supreme consequences for the power of sin in our lives. No
passage is more eloquent on this matter than Romans 6. 'Don't
you know,' Paul argues, 'that all of us who were baptized into
Christ Jesus were baptized into his death? We were therefore
buried with him through baptism into death in order that, just
as Christ was raised from the dead through the glory of the
Father, we too may live a new life' (Rom. 6:3-4).

John Owen once remarked that every pastoral difficulty
amounts to either persuading non-Christians that they are
sinners, or persuading Christians that they have died to sin and
are no longer under its dominion. Some Christians were,
apparently, arguing that since God's grace was so superabun-
dant, it did not matter much how they lived since God was
bound to forgive them. This was, of course, a cheapening of
grace and a denial of the Christian life. Paul's response is to say
that the believer does not go on living in sin because he has
died to sin. Christians have a new identity: they are those who
have 'died to sin' (Rom. 6:2).

It is interesting to note the metaphors for sin that the apostle
uses: sin is a king who reigns, a tyrant who dominates his
slaves, a general who commands his artillery, an employer
who pays the wages of death. Sin is a reigning power in the
lives of unbelievers. And Paul wants us to know that Christ has
died, not only *for* sin, but *to* sin: 'The death he died, he died to
sin once for all' (Rom. 6:10). Christ not only took upon himself
the punishment that sin deserved, but he also took on its power.
He faced up to its threatening, dominating influence and
defeated it. He was, we might say, stronger than sin's power.

Every claim that sin makes is exhausted in Christ. In Christ the old man is crucified.

Everything that we were in Adam is dead and what we are now is something entirely different and new. We are, therefore, no longer dominated by what we were in Adam but by what we are in Christ — the Christ who has risen in power! Think of yourselves as dead men who have come to life and act accordingly: 'Therefore do not let sin reign in your mortal body so that you obey its evil desires. Do not offer the parts of your body to sin, as instruments of wickedness, but rather offer yourselves to God, as those who have been brought from death to life; and offer the parts of your body to him as instruments of righteousness' (Rom. 6:12-13). Who are we? We are those who are 'in Christ' and this has the profoundest implications for the way we live. As Sinclair Ferguson puts it, 'The knowledge of our union with Christ provides us with great dignity. As I look at myself I see failure, sin, sometimes shame and disgrace. But that is neither the ultimate nor the whole truth about me as a Christian. No! I am united to Christ, a joint heir of his riches, a child of God. Knowing this to be the real truth about me lends grace and power to my life.'[6]

It also helps us appreciate *what we should be*. As those who are 'dead to sin', we have no right to let sin have any influence in our lives at all. Influence it most certainly does have, of course, and even though its power is seriously curtailed, its power is nevertheless awesome and our Christian lives are to be spent clipping its wings. Believers are to 'put to death the misdeeds of the body' (Rom. 8:13). Our union with Christ provides us with the incentive to destroy every rising of sin in our lives, because it tells us that we are able to do it. Paul did not believe in sinless perfection; he was quite clear that believers will be troubled by sin for the whole of their lives. Equally, he was not a defeatist. 'Grace reigns!' was his slogan, and by it he meant us to be confident in the power at our disposal in putting sin to death. The issue for the apostle was simple enough: do I want Christ and his way more than I want sin and its bitter fruit?

The strongest motive for crucifying sin in our lives is that Christ died to put away our sin and to bring us into union with himself: Christ died for sin so that we might no longer go on living in sin (Rom. 8:4). This is implied in Jesus' description of the Christian life in terms of the union between a branch and the trunk of the vine: 'Remain in me, and I will remain in you. No branch can bear fruit by itself; it must remain in the vine. Neither can you bear fruit unless you remain in me. I am the vine; you are the branches. If a man remains in me, and I in him, he will bear much fruit; apart from me you can do nothing' (John 15:4-5). Only as we continue to remain 'in Christ' can we live the life God intends us to live. 'When we experience external temptation to sin, or feel the power of sinful desires from within, we are to resort to the cross of Christ, where that sin was condemned in Christ. We are to say to ourselves, "How can I possibly live to this sin, sow to this flesh, when my Saviour died for the specific purpose of delivering me from sin?" To do so would be to trample under my feet the blood of the covenant he shed for me.'[7]

It also helps us appreciate *what may happen to us*. We share in his death as well as his resurrection. Every Christian is called upon to take up a cross and follow after Christ (Matt. 16:24; Mark 8:34; Luke 9:23). Carrying one's cross in Jesus' day was required of those whom society had condemned, whose rights were forfeit, and who were now being led to their execution. The cross they carried was the instrument of death. If we are serious about wanting to live for God, we shall have to take seriously God's call to suffering; it is a mark of Christian discipleship. We always carry around in our body the dying of the Lord Jesus, so that the life of Jesus may also be revealed in our mortal body (2 Cor. 4:10-12). Death works in us, so that life may work in others.

No one saw this better than Amy Carmichael, when she wrote:

> Lord crucified, Oh, mark thy holy cross
> On motive, preference, all fond desire
> On that which self, in any form, inspires,
> Set thou this sign of loss.
> And when the touch of death is here and there displayed
> On things most precious in our eyes.
> Let us not wonder; let us see the answer to this prayer.

Union with Christ assures us of ultimate glory. We live and die in Christ. Even in death both body and soul, though temporarily torn apart from each other, remain united to Christ. 'Could anything illustrate the indissolubility of union with Christ more plainly than the fact that this union is not severed in death?' asks John Murray.[8] Every stride in gospel holiness is an encouragement to long for that day when, in Christ, we shall be resurrected; when these bodies of humiliation are made like the body of his glory. And Paul seems to contemplate that this will serve as the beginning of a relationship that will last for ever and ever: 'And so we will be with the Lord for ever' (1 Thess. 4:17). We need to develop a longing for it. Other-worldliness has always been a siren call of reformed theology. The only way to live in this world is by 'looking to Jesus' who himself looked for the 'joy set before him' (Heb. 12:2). It is vividly expressed in the *Heidelberg Catechism*:

Question. What is your only comfort in life and in death?

Answer. That I am not my own, but belong — body and
soul, in life and in death — to my faithful Saviour Jesus
Christ.

The Counsellor

The disciples in the upper room were afraid. They did not
understand what was happening. 'Lord,' cried Thomas, 'we
don't know where you are going...' (John 14:5). In response,
Jesus promised the Holy Spirit whom he describes as 'another
Counsellor to be with you for ever' (14:16; cf. 14:26; 15:26;
16:7). The Holy Spirit carries on the work of counselling
which began with Jesus. And the Spirit's counselling ministry
began in its fulness on Pentecost morning, following Jesus'
ascension (Acts 2:1-4).

What is the significance of the term 'Counsellor'? The
word has several plausible translations, including advocate,
helper, strengthener and (a mere transliteration) *paraclete*. In
the forefront lies the idea of one who comes to our aid in times
of trouble. This was what the disciples needed to hear in the
upper room, for they were afraid. But they had no cause to be,
for the Holy Spirit would spring to their defence after Jesus had
gone. But against whom would the Spirit defend them? Who
is their enemy?

What Jesus was alluding to in the upper room was the work
of Satan. He had already entered the heart of Judas (John
13:27) and had threatened to undo the testimony of the others
(cf. Luke 22:31). The disciples needed to prepare for a life of
spiritual warfare. Satan hates Christians because he first of all
hates God. A fallen angel, he lives to wreck and dismantle
everything that God has made. When God makes something
good, Satan keeps pace scheming ways to undo his handiwork.
An entire army of demons are led by one who is 'king over

them the angel of the Abyss, whose name in Hebrew is Abaddon, and in Greek, Apollyon' (Rev. 9:11) — both names meaning 'destroyer'. Vicious and mean, Satan seeks every opportunity to devour those who claim to belong to Christ. Like a roaring lion he prowls around for opportunities to strike unawares with lethal ferocity. And who can possibly help us in such times? The Holy Spirit!

The precise form of the encouragement given by Jesus needs to be noticed. The Holy Spirit whom Jesus promised had been the source of his own help throughout his ministry on earth. As God's Servant, the Father had given him the fulness of the Spirit (cf. Isa. 42:1). At every step of the journey, Jesus met the full ferocity of Satan's attacks by recourse to the Spirit's help and advocacy. The one promised to the disciples is the one whom Jesus had intimately known throughout the days of his incarnate life. In a sense, he was promising the disciples the ministry of a 'friend', his best Friend! It is as though Jesus is saying to the disciples, 'I am going away, but someone very special will come and help you. He has been with me every day. He was with me when I was a little child. He was with me when I began my ministry. He was with me in the wilderness. He will be with me as I go to the cross.'

The relevance of all this should not be difficult to grasp. After all, Jesus had known the Spirit's help even when Satan threw everything he had against him. In our case, Satan need not try that hard! We fall at the mere suggestion of his coming! But such is the Spirit's ability and power that even the combined ferocity of hell could not bring an accusation against Jesus Christ. If the Holy Spirit can survive that, dealing with our battles will be no problem to him. This is what John means when he reminds his readers, 'The one who is in you is greater than the one who is in the world' (1 John 4:4).

The Home-Maker

Few descriptions of the ministry of the Holy Spirit are more sublime than this one: that he is the supreme home-maker. Speaking of a joint ministry with the Holy Spirit, Jesus says to the disciples: 'We will come to him and make our home with him' (John 14:23). The Holy Spirit sets up home by coming to dwell in our hearts. 'You know him,' Jesus says, 'for he lives with you and will be in you' (John 14:17). Paul asks the question: 'Do you not know that your body is a temple of the Holy Spirit, who is in you, whom you have received from God?' And then he draws the conclusion: 'You are not your own' (1 Cor. 6:19).

Using the same idea of a temple, the apostle writes to the Ephesians, suggesting that believers are 'a holy temple in the Lord ... built together to become a dwelling in which God lives by his Spirit' (Eph. 2:21-22). The word 'dwelling' is meant to convey the idea that the Holy Spirit 'settles down' and makes his home in the hearts of those who know God. What it means is made clearer in the following chapter, when Paul equates the coming of the Holy Spirit into our hearts with the coming of Christ himself as he prays that God 'may strengthen you with power through his Spirit in your inner being, so that Christ may dwell [same word] in your hearts through faith' (Eph. 3:16-17). Paul is concerned that we should know two things: that we might be empowered by the Spirit (3:16-17a); and that we might grasp the limitless, multi-faceted dimensions of the love of Christ (3:17b-19). The presence of the Holy Spirit aids us through every conceivable circumstance by focusing our gaze upon Jesus Christ.

'The Holy Spirit', Paul informs his friend Timothy, 'lives in us' (2 Tim. 1:14), conveying the idea of someone living in a house! The thought is breathtaking! There is no moment in which God is absent from us. Even though Jesus was going away, in reality he would be closer to them as a result of his going than he ever was before. He now dwells in us for the purposes of fellowship. He is closer to us than a brother (cf. Prov. 18:24).

Though we do not have Jesus with us physically, we have something even better: we have the Holy Spirit in our hearts. He shines a light on the face of Jesus in heaven, reminding us of our union with him, and our eventual presence with him where he is. For now, we have work to do, for which certain gifts are needed in order to accomplish it. To this we must turn in the next chapter. The ascension of Jesus initiated a deeper ministry of the Holy Spirit in our hearts.

5.
Distributing gifts to the church

The church, if it is to function properly, needs certain skills and abilities. It is one of the more colourful aspects of the Greek language that the word for 'gift' and for 'grace' is the same: *charis*. Every gift in the church is given freely and undeservedly by God. The distribution is not according to merit; it is solely due to the wisdom of the giver.

Every Christian is gifted in some way: 'But to each one of us grace has been given as Christ apportioned it' (Eph. 4:7). The verse could equally be read: 'But to each one of us a gift has been given...' Gifts are graces; they are freely distributed to each one of us in accordance with God's love for his people individually and his church corporately. In this sense, every Christian is a charismatic. This does not mean that every Christian possesses a dominant, forceful personality. Nor does it mean that every Christian speaks in tongues, or has the gift of prophecy, or engages in a frenetic kind of worship.

To say that the church is charismatic is to reclaim a biblical concept that has been lost to the excesses of certain branches of the church. It is merely to state a biblical idea: that every Christian possesses spiritual gifts and that the church depends on these gifts for its survival and growth. Those who make up Christ's church are not in themselves powerful and talented.

The ministry which the church needs for its effectiveness springs from the distribution of gifts to the church by the Holy Spirit. Some of these gifts were meant to survive for only a brief period of time. The gifts of prophecy and tongues, for example, are intimately linked with revelation and the gift of the Bible to the church as an inerrant account of all that God wants us to know. But other gifts remain: wisdom, knowledge, teaching, counselling, government, leadership, serving, comforting, exhorting, liberality, administration.

The distribution of these gifts to the church is intimately connected with the victory of Christ at Calvary. The ascension is portrayed in the Bible as an example of what happened in ancient times following a battle: the victor would march through his home city with the spoils of battle on display and these would be brought into 'the temple of the idol'. Sometimes, the victorious leader would throw some of the spoils to his adoring crowds, thereby sharing with them the spoils of his victory. That is what Paul means when he writes to the Colossians, 'And having disarmed the powers and authorities, he made a public spectacle of them, triumphing over them by the cross' (Col. 2:15). After Jesus ascended into heaven in triumph and sat at the right hand of God, one of the first things he did was to pour out the Holy Spirit and share with his people the spoils of war. He gave to his church what she needed to fulfil her mandate.

It is to this that Paul refers in Ephesians 4:7-12:

But to each one of us grace has been given as Christ apportioned it. This is why it says:

'When he ascended on high,
   he led captives in his train
   and gave gifts to men.'

(What does 'he ascended' mean except that he also descended to the lower, earthly regions? He who descended is the very one who ascended higher than all the heavens, in order to fill the whole universe.) It was he who gave some to be apostles, some to be prophets, some to be evangelists, and some to be pastors and teachers, to prepare God's people for works of service, so that the body of Christ may be built up.

Jesus Christ — the Head of the church

That sermon is most useful that has most of Christ in it. So said a certain Puritan preacher, and he was right. Paul would have agreed with the sentiment for in this passage he finds himself asserting Christ at a point where we might not have expected him to. Having written that 'To each one of us grace has been given as Christ apportioned it' (Eph. 4:7), we might have expected him to enumerate for us what these gifts might be. Before he does, however, he inserts what Bible translations have universally regarded as a parenthesis:

> When he ascended on high,
>   he led captives in his train
>   and gave gifts to men
>
> (Eph. 4:8).

He wants us to catch the significance of prophecy and miracle in the distribution of gifts to the church: prophecy, in that the church and its ministry are not an afterthought, but something foretold in the Old Testament; miracle, in that the gifts distributed are a direct consequence of Christ's ascension to God's right hand.

The quotation itself comes from Psalm 68:18. As often happens when we cite a passage from the Bible, we tend to paraphrase. This should pose no problems as far as our belief in the inerrancy of Scripture is concerned. It is, then, not an exact quotation: Paul substitutes the word 'gave' for the original 'received'. But no real issue is at stake. To receive and pass on is part and parcel of the same action, and Paul is concerned to emphasize what we now have from Christ.

The psalm is a celebration of God's help in rescuing Israel from Egypt. It speaks of God coming down and delivering them through the Red Sea, and having shown them his power and grace, returning to heaven again. Paul has no trouble whatsoever in reading 'Jesus' for YHWH — the covenant God of Israel! The ascension was Jesus' public demonstration of victory over the devil. He led captivity captive. He triumphed over his enemies. He displays the spoils of his victory by throwing some of them down at the feet of his own people. He shares with us his glorious conquest. No one has ever achieved so much, or given so much.

The essential unity of the body of Christ

Seven times in the adjoining section, the apostle has emphasized the word 'one' (4:4-6), the main point being that 'There is one body' (4:4). Every Christian belongs to the one body of Christ. We are saved in exactly the same way: 'You are all sons of God through faith in Christ Jesus' (Gal. 3:26). In a large family there are some who are boys and some who are girls, but they are all children. They share the same parents. In essence, then, we are united. Of course, in practice this unity can be broken, and often is. Just as children fall out with each other, even though they remain brothers and sisters, so God's children display quarrelsome tendencies: hence Jesus' prayer, 'I pray also … that all of them may be one' (John 17:20-21), and Paul's exhortation: 'Make every effort to keep the unity of the Spirit through the bond of peace' (Eph. 4:3; cf. Rom. 15:5). And how is this unity maintained? By love: 'And over all these virtues put on love, which binds them all together in perfect unity' (Col. 3:14). We are one in Christ even though on the surface we often appear to be at loggerheads.

The diversity of the body of Christ

'But to each one of us grace has been given as Christ apportioned it' (Eph. 4:7). Jesus, having ascended and taken his seat at the right hand of the Father as King and Head of the church, now distributes gifts to his people. The gifts he distributes differ according to each individual member of his body. The distribution is not arbitrary, but wholly dependent on the wisdom of Christ. The differing gifts in no way call into question the unity of the body or the unity of the one who distributes them.

This is something Paul alludes to again in writing to the Corinthians about a similar issue: 'There are different kinds of gifts, but the same Spirit. There are different kinds of service, but the same Lord. There are different kinds of working, but the same God works all of them in all men' (1 Cor. 12:4-6). The multi-faceted wisdom of God is seen in the specific allocation of gifts God makes to each individual member of his body. 'Each one should use whatever gift he has received to serve others, faithfully administering God's grace in its various forms' (1 Peter 4:10). 'Just as each of us has one body with many members, and these members do not all have the same function, so in Christ we who are many form one body, and each member belongs to all the others. We have different gifts, according to the grace given us. If a man's gift is prophesying, let him use it in proportion to his faith' (Rom. 12:4-6). It is not just preachers and evangelists who are gifted; all Christians are. It is certainly true that the ascended Lord donates gifts to the church in the form of men called and equipped for the ministries of apostle, prophet, evangelist and pastor-teacher. But through them, he also encourages every Christian to exercise a role of ministry of one kind or another.

Building up the body of Christ

To what purpose are these gifts distributed amongst God's people? Paul is insistent: all gifts are intended for the growth and edification of the church. 'It was he who gave some to be apostles, some to be prophets, some to be evangelists, and some to be pastors and teachers, to prepare God's people for works of service, so that the body of Christ may be built up' (Eph. 4:11-12).

Modern students of English are, sadly, spared the technicalities of grammar, but everyone should know the difference a comma makes. The Authorized Version, by inserting a comma where, according to some, none was needed, made Paul say the opposite of what he intended. By inserting a comma after the word saints — 'And he gave some, apostles; and some, prophets; and some, evangelists; and some, pastors and teachers; for the perfecting of the saints, for the work of the ministry, for the edifying of the body of Christ' (Eph. 4:11-12) — they made it sound as though Paul restricted the work of 'the ministry' to these official delegates.[1] The case for its inclusion is strong: Paul has been talking about very specific gifts: apostles, prophets, evangelists, pastor-teachers — gifts which belonged to only some believers specifically chosen by God. This ministry of service *(diakonia)*, which Paul now mentions, is one which elsewhere in the New Testament seems to be associated with specific individuals: Paul himself (2 Cor. 3:8,9; 4:1; 5:18; 6:3; Rom. 11:13) and his co-workers, Stephanas (1 Cor. 16:15) and Archippus (Col. 4:17).[2]

However, the omission of the comma, thus making the gifts of apostle, prophet, evangelist and pastor-teacher a means of encouraging the individual members of the church to fulfil their ministries, has gained increasing favour of late. Attention has been drawn to the fact that a different preposition is used between the first and second phrases: 'for *(pros)* the perfecting of the saints, for *(eis)* the work of the ministry, for *(eis)* the edifying of the body of Christ'. Of greater significance is the fact that in the larger context Paul is stressing the distribution of gifts to the entire body: 'But *to each one of us* grace has been given...' (Eph. 4:7, emphasis added); 'From him *the whole body*, joined and held together by every supporting ligament, grows and builds itself up in love, *as each part does its work*' (Eph. 4:16, emphasis added).[3]

This is no way undermines the role of those called to specific tasks of leadership and ministry within the church (paid or otherwise); rather, it is to emphasize that every Christian has something to contribute to the building up of the body of Christ. The church ought to have a zero unemployment rate.

Building up the body of Christ implies that gifts were never meant for mere individual gratification. Self-indulgence is wrong at any time, particularly so in the church of Christ. The Corinthians were cock-a-hoop over the extent of their gifts, even to the point of despising others within the church and, in particular, visitors who came supposedly to help them. Gifted they may have been, but they were also carnal and childish (1 Cor. 3:1-4; 5:1-13; 6:1-8; 11:17-22). They had missed the fundamental point: gifts are meant to aid others in growing up in Christ. Far from encouraging maturity, the Corinthians were using their gifts as means of one-upmanship. They were essentially rude, as Paul makes clear by contrasting the way of love with the way of the Corinthians (1 Cor. 13). Without love, the greatest gifts imaginable are nothing. They may have regarded themselves as 'spiritually gifted' (1 Cor. 14:37), but some of them were 'ignorant of God' and Paul adds, 'I say this to your shame' (1 Cor. 15:34).

Gifts are meant to edify. They 'build up' (cf. 1 Cor. 14:3-5,12,26; Eph. 4:12,16). Their use encourages individual Christians and the body of Christ collectively to grow up in Christ. Their use by the church is nothing more or less than Christ himself working in and through his people, thereby bringing glory to his Father in heaven. As J. I. Packer puts it, 'From heaven Christ uses Christians as his mouth, his hands, his feet, even his smile; it is through us, his people, that he speaks and acts, meets, loves, and saves here and now in this world.'[4] Christ had never been to Ephesus, and yet Paul insists that he had preached there. What did he mean? It was through the preaching and teaching of Paul that '*He* came and preached peace to you...' (Eph. 2:17, emphasis added).

When you drop round to see a lonely member of the church and chat, supply an elderly person with a hot meal, or write a letter of encouragement to a discouraged soldier of Christ, you meet their needs. In fact, Christ meets their needs through you. That is what Paul means when he says with such confidence: 'And my God will meet all your needs according to his glorious riches in Christ Jesus' (Phil. 4:19). It is not, as is so often thought, a statement of faith in supernatural intervention; it is, rather, an affirmation of Paul's confidence in Christ's body, the church, to fulfil its obligations and responsibilities. It is just as Jesus said: 'Whatever you did for one of the least of these brothers of mine, you did for me' (Matt. 25:40).

What gifts?

What are the gifts? The New Testament provides us with three lists of spiritual gifts: Romans 12:3-13; 1 Corinthians 12 and Ephesians 4:7-15. They are not meant to be exhaustive. In 1 Corinthians 12:1-6, Paul uses three words to describe the gifts. They are *charismata* (12:4), emphasizing their origin in God's gracious distribution (their presence owes itself to nothing in ourselves, and everything to God); they are *diakonia* (12:5), a word which captures the service element of the gifts (they are meant for helping others grow); they are *pneumatika* (12:6), the word *pneumos*, 'Spirit', conveying the powerful energy of the Holy Spirit that each gift demonstrates.

Essentially, all the gifts are of two types: gifts of speech and gifts of practical helpfulness. A careful examination of the order of gifts reveals that Paul makes little or no distinction between the level of importance he gives to each individual gift. Thus in Romans 12:6-8 he inserts between such gifts as prophecy, teaching and exhorting, such gifts as serving, giving, ruling and showing mercy.

Amid all the obscurities relating to New Testament gifts, one perennial problem exists: are all of them extant in the church today? It appears that some gifts were so closely allied to the apostles and their specific function as instruments of revelation that their continued existence is unwarrantable. They were 'the things that mark an apostle' (2 Cor. 12:12). Through them God gave the church an inerrant Bible, his final word concerning all that Christians need know to guide them safely to heaven.[5] Thus, for example, the offices of apostle and prophet (two gifts mentioned in Ephesians 4:11) are earlier referred to as the foundation on which the church is built (Eph. 2:20). The assumption must surely be that, whilst these two gifts were current at the time Paul wrote this letter to Ephesus, they would soon be hidden by the superstructure of the church

growing and expanding on the basis of the completed revelation of Scripture left behind by the apostles and prophets of
the early church. The two most common gifts associated with
the apostles and prophets (tongues and prophecy — the latter
being by far and away more important) seem to disappear as
the New Testament days progressed. Thus, by the time Paul
comes to write his final epistles (Titus and 2 Timothy), the
gifts of prophecy and tongues are nowhere mentioned.

> Is it to be concluded that these gifts related to new
> revelation still were functioning widely at this late date
> in the apostolic age, since no command forbidding them
> has been issued? The precise opposite seems to be the
> case, particularly in the light of Paul's extensive re-
> marks regarding the phenomenon that appropriately
> could substitute for the unending continuation of these
> revelational gifts. In his last letters to Timothy and Titus,
> Paul employs a number of phrases underscoring the
> importance of holding to the sound teaching that has
> been provided them...
>
> There is 'the deposit' of truth, there is 'sound doc-
> trine', there is 'the tradition', there is 'the faith', there is
> 'the trustworthy message'. It is not that there was no
> awareness earlier of a 'deposit' of faith, a body of
> doctrines to be believed, for references can be found in
> Paul's earlier writings to this kind of phenomenon (cf.
> 2 Thess. 2:15; 3:6). But the completeness, the suffi-
> ciency of a tradition of teaching that had been received
> came only at the end of the apostolic age.[6]

The cessation of certain revelatory gifts should not in any
way lessen the importance of those gifts which remain. They
are to be valued and cultivated. Without them the church is im-
measurably impoverished. To the great surprise of Corinthian

believers who traded in one-upmanship, Paul stressed that every single Christian had value in the kingdom of God. Every believer is baptized in the Spirit, and thereby equipped for service. And in particular, the gifts are meant 'for the profit of all' (1 Cor. 12:7, NKJV).

It is easy to abuse the gifts God gives. How quickly we can forget that each one of them is a gracious bestowal of the Almighty! Some Christians sneer and look down at others less gifted (in their estimation) than themselves. Some are too quick to conclude that they have no need of the ministries of others (1 Cor. 12:21). In fact, God takes special care and interest in those less gifted! (1 Cor. 12:23). I think, for example, of how protective a mother can be of her child who is less able than some of her other children. 'This is my special son,' a mother said to me once, introducing a child with Down's Syndrome. She really meant it. He was very special and dear to her.

Some Christians may feel (and be made to feel) inferior: 'If the foot should say, "Because I am not a hand, I do not belong to the body," it would not for that reason cease to be part of the body' (1 Cor. 12:15). By no means! The eye is as important as the ear (v. 17). John Milton, reflecting on his own blindness, and the feeling of uselessness that dogged him, put it eloquently:

> When I consider how much my light is spent,
> E're half my days, in this dark world and wide,
> And that one Talent which is death to hide,
> Lodg'd with me useless, though my Soul more bent
> To serve therewith my maker, and present
> My true account, lest He returning chide;
> 'Doth God exact day-labour, light deny'd?'
> I fondly ask; But patience, to prevent
> That murmur, soon replies, 'God doth not need

> Either man's work or his own gifts. Who best
> Bear his mild yoke, they serve him best, his State
> Is Kingly. Thousands at his bidding speed
> And post o'er land and Ocean without rest:
> They also serve who only stand and wait.'

The purpose of the gifts Christ distributes to the church from his ascension throne is that the church might be 'built up' (Eph. 4:12). That is the goal of all we do: that we might grow in grace and mature in Christ. Like newborn babes we are meant to grow (cf. John 3:3; Rom. 8:15; 1 Peter 2:2).

There is nothing worse than Christians who never seem to grow. Or, putting it another way, one of the most encouraging things in the Christian life is to meet someone whom we have not seen or heard from for many years, and to see the level of spiritual maturity that has been attained. There is nothing quite like it! Yet how rare it is! Too often Christians never seem to make any progress at all! And sometimes they regress into a state of backslidden lethargy and indifference to spiritual things.

We need to catch a fresh vision of the ascended Christ. Most of our troubles arise when we take our eyes off him. Too easily we find ourselves immersed in what this world offers, rather than what Christ longs to give us. Every letter that Paul wrote had as its focus some aspect of the person and work of Christ.

Have you taken this matter seriously? Have you thanked God for the gifts that you possess? Are you using them to further the growth and development of other Christians in the church? Do we see our lives as a service devoted to the Master? Are we prepared to die daily to self-interest and to labour for the advancement of the body of Christ? That is the reason why Christ died. It is the work to which he now calls us from his throne on high.

Perhaps you are tempted to share your talents with a select few, an élite band of carefully chosen, non-threatening individuals. Perhaps you have chosen them because they flatter you. We have always to examine our motives, even in the most spiritual matters. The ascended Christ intends us to share our lives with the weak and troubled, the disconsolate and difficult. The pattern is shown us: while we were yet sinners, Christ died and rose again for us. The Lord shows his pity to the just and the unjust. Perhaps, if we had the choice, we would limit the bestowal of our kindness to those who will show us gratitude and respect in return. But in doing so, we shall have moved away from the pattern of our Saviour. Our lives are meant to be lived for the sake of others.

6.
Jesus the home-maker

In the last chapter we touched on the aspect of the Spirit's work which involves making a home in our hearts as the personal representative agent of the ascended Christ. In this work the Spirit is reflecting the work of Jesus himself, for he, too, is a home-maker: 'In my Father's house are many rooms; if it were not so, I would have told you. I am going there to prepare a place for you. And if I go and prepare a place for you, I will come back and take you to be with me that you also may be where I am' (John 14:2-3).

It is important for us to note what Jesus is doing in these chapters that make up his Farewell Discourse in the upper room. Many have noted that whilst the other Gospels show us Christ's body, John shows us his soul. What is evident in these chapters is the way Jesus seeks to pastor the disciples. In both the opening and closing remarks of John 14, Jesus says to them: 'Do not let your hearts be troubled' (John 14:1,27). Within a few hours he was to be crucified, but the focus of his concern is not himself, but his disciples. His own problems are pushed aside and those of his followers are ministered to. To the very end he shows us that he came, not to be ministered to, but to serve.

If the disciples were troubled, so was Jesus. It is interesting to note that the very same verb is used to describe the emotions of the disciples at this point and those of Jesus himself. At the sight of Mary and others weeping over the death of Lazarus, we read that Jesus 'was deeply moved in spirit and troubled' (John 11:33). As he dwelt on the prospect of his coming death, we are told that he cried out in prayer to his Father in heaven: 'Now my heart is troubled...' (John 12:27). As he foretold the betrayal of Judas and the demonic activity that lay behind it, we further read that 'Jesus was troubled in spirit' (John 13:21). As one who is clearly sympathetic to our weaknesses (cf. Heb. 4:15), it is touching that Jesus seeks to minister to the sense of unease ('trouble') felt by the disciples in the upper room.

Two immediate reasons explain the unease felt by the disciples: the first was Jesus' prediction of Judas' betrayal and Peter's imminent denial; and the second, Jesus' imminent departure.

Failing disciples

It is a mistake to think that the betrayal of Judas came to the disciples as anything but a shock. They had not expected it from him. Indeed, when Jesus first predicted that someone would deny him, the 'disciples stared at one another, at a loss to know which of them he meant' (13:22). Judas was not immediately singled out as the most likely suspect. Evidently there was little in his character to suggest to the rest of the disciples that he was the obvious candidate for such treachery. Indeed, such was their confusion that Peter motioned to John, who was closest to Jesus at the time, that he might ask Jesus which of them Jesus had in mind. 'Lord, who is it?' John asked (13:25). Even after it had become evident that Judas was the betrayer, and after he had left the room to begin his dark work, the disciples were still clearly shaken by it all. If Judas, one of their own, and with whom they had shared in ministry, could apostatize in this way, perhaps they could too! 'I beat my body and make it my slave,' Paul wrote, 'so that after I have preached to others, I myself will not be disqualified for the prize' (1 Cor. 9:27). No wonder they were troubled.

Not only had Jesus warned of Judas' betrayal, he had also given clear indications that another of their band would let him down. Though Peter's denial of Jesus is not in the same league as Judas' betrayal, it is, nevertheless a serious matter. In denying any knowledge of Jesus in the high priest's courtyard, not once but three times, Peter had fallen victim to the opinions of men. This was a weakness in Peter's character that revealed itself with some degree of regularity. The death, resurrection and ascension of Christ changed Peter's life. The man became a 'rock' as Jesus had predicted. What people saw and heard on the Day of Pentecost was a different man to the one portrayed in the Gospels. And yet, similarities remained. Peter was afraid of what certain people might be saying about him. In Antioch, years after Pentecost, Peter once again fell victim to the prejudices of what the apostle Paul called 'the circumcision party'. These were men who insisted that table fellowship with Gentiles still soiled those Jews, even Christian Jews, who took part in it. These were influential folk and Peter was loath to be out of favour with them. Consequently, he withdrew his fellowship with uncircumcised Gentile believers and earned from Paul a stern and public rebuke (Gal. 2:11-14). Peter had once again become captive to the opinions of men.

The disciples in the upper room were understandably nervous. If Peter's faith was as fragile as this, would theirs fare any better? Would they also deny him when the pressures mounted? Would they persevere in his absence? These are questions that we need to ask ourselves. Will our faith hold up in a moment of testing? We know all too well that God does not promise to keep us from failure. He occasionally allows us to fall so as to teach us important lessons that can be learned in no other way. But it is also true that apart from God's help we would find ourselves falling constantly. Peter must have reflected often on that truth. Almost the very first words he wrote to the church contained some thoughts along these very lines. We are 'shielded by God's power,' he wrote, adding that it is 'through faith' (1 Peter 1:5). The failures were all too real; they were a hindrance to Peter's growth in grace. Yet despite them, even through them, God moulded Peter into one of his giants. But all of this was far from the thoughts of the disciples in that upper room. All they could hear at this point was Jesus' prediction that, in his very hour of need, they would let him down. And if Peter, then why not all of them?

Forsaken disciples

Of even greater significance for the disciples in the upper room were the words that Jesus spoke in predicting Peter's denial: 'My children, I will be with you only a little longer. You will look for me, and just as I told the Jews, so I tell you now: Where I am going, you cannot come' (John 13:33). 'Lord, where are you going?' Peter had asked (13:36).

We have already noted in the previous chapter that Jesus sought to minister to their fear of his departure by promising them 'another Counsellor', the Holy Spirit. That was later in the course of the evening. But for now another consequence of his going away is to be underlined. He is going to make a home for the disciples.

The remedy of faith

As he sought to minister to the disciples' fear, he urged them to trust in God (14:1).[1] What we have here, wrote Bishop J. C.

Ryle, is 'a precious remedy against an old disease. That
disease is trouble of heart. That remedy is faith.'[2]

Trust in God

Jesus is teaching a fundamental lesson about the nature of the
Christian life. It is lived out, not on beds of ease but on
battlefields. If the enemy is to be resisted — and Satan's
presence in the upper room is something John notes (13:2,27)
— believers must resist him by drawing strength from everything they know of God. They must resort to prayer. They must
also stick to God through thick and thin, refusing to allow
themselves to be crushed by the troubles that come their way.
It is interesting to note how Peter warns his readers to beware
of becoming troubled, for Satan often lurks alongside such
fear: 'Be self-controlled and alert. Your enemy the devil
prowls around like a roaring lion looking for someone to
devour. Resist him...' (1 Peter 5:8-9). And how are we to resist
Satan? By casting all our anxiety upon God (5:7), and by
'standing firm in the faith' (5:9).

This is, after all, what saints have always done and Hebrews
11 supplies us with a long list of harassed believers who fought
against all kinds of hostility, not least the fear and trouble in
their own hearts, by exercising faith. And what is faith?
Hebrews 11:1 provides us with as comprehensive a definition
as any constructed since: 'Now faith is being sure of what we
hope for and certain of what we do not see.' It is not that we are
certain about the quality and vitality of our faith; of that we can
have no certainty. Faith is being certain that what God says, he
will do. Thus Abraham 'considered him [God] faithful who
had made the promise' (Heb. 11:11). It is not faith in our faith.
It is faith in God's objective, unbreakable Word.

The disciples must trust what God had said to them. And
what was that? At its heart was God's covenantal promise to

be their God, within which relationship he would care for, provide for, nurture and protect his people. He had found a way to save his people from their sins and the presence of Jesus was proof of it. Having rescued them, he was not about to let them go. It is the faith that sings at the heart of the best-known psalm in Israel and the church today:

> The LORD is my shepherd, I shall not be in want.
>> He makes me lie down in green pastures,
> he leads me beside quiet waters,
>> he restores my soul.
> He guides me in paths of righteousness
>> for his name's sake.
> Even though I walk
>> through the valley of the shadow of death,
> I will fear no evil,
>> for you are with me;
> your rod and your staff,
>> they comfort me.
> You prepare a table before me
>> in the presence of my enemies.
> You anoint my head with oil;
>> my cup overflows.
> Surely goodness and love will follow me
>> all the days of my life,
> and I will dwell in the house of the LORD
>> for ever

                                                    (Ps. 23).

'Trust in me'

Not only does Jesus bid his disciples trust in God; he bids them also to trust in himself. And the way he puts this suggests that he has no difficulty whatsoever in placing himself alongside

God as an equal! 'Trust in God; trust also in me' (14:1). It is one of the staggering features about Jesus' ministry that he urged folk not simply to put their trust in God, but to do that by putting their trust in himself. At the beginning of the twentieth century, Gresham Machen fought a courageous and lonely battle against liberalism in the church. At the heart of his objection to the modern theology of his day was the tendency, as he saw it, of regarding Jesus as an *example* of faith rather than the *object* of faith.

Writing of Paul's attitude to Christ, Machen asked, 'What, then, was the attitude of this representative of the first Christian generation toward Jesus of Nazareth? The answer cannot be at all in doubt. The apostle Paul clearly stood always toward Jesus in a truly religious relationship. Jesus was not for Paul merely an example of faith; He was primarily the object of faith. The religion of Paul did not consist in having faith in God like the faith which Jesus had in God; it consisted rather in having faith *in Jesus*.'[3] This is precisely what Jesus is saying to the disciples in the upper room; they are to trust him.

But what specifically were the disciples to believe concerning Jesus? If faith is being certain that what God says, he will do, what has Jesus promised to do? Already he has told the disciples: 'Do not be afraid of those who kill the body but cannot kill the soul. Rather, be afraid of the One who can destroy both soul and body in hell' (Matt. 10:28). 'Just as Moses lifted up the snake in the desert, so the Son of Man must be lifted up' (John 3:14). 'I am the good shepherd. The good shepherd lays down his life for the sheep' (John 10:11). 'I give them eternal life, and they shall never perish; no one can snatch them out of my hand. My Father, who has given them to me, is greater than all; no one can snatch them out of my Father's hand' (John 10:28-29).

These were things the disciples had already heard. Now he adds something else: 'I am going there to prepare a place for you... I will come back and take you to be with me that you also may be where I am' (John 14:2-3).

The place to which Jesus refers already exists; but it is not yet ready for his disciples to occupy; Jesus has to go and prepare it for them. The crucifixion, resurrection and ascension were all necessary to make heaven habitable for Jesus' disciples. Several features of heaven now come into view.

Heaven

What is heaven like? The question is often asked and most of us at some time or another have wondered about it.

1. Heaven is a place

A trio of words describe what Jesus has in view for those whom he loves. First, it is a 'place' (John 14:3) which signals a real, literal location. We all remember the jibe of the Russian cosmonaut who, on an early space flight, told the listening world, and his communistic audience back home in particular, that he had looked out into space and heaven wasn't there.

More disturbingly, some evangelicals are currently arguing that we should think of heaven more as a condition than a location. Some parts of the book of Revelation reinforce the point that heaven is depicted in Scripture by apocalyptic images which defy reality and depict a state of blessedness, rather than a geographical location. Some have gone to the extent of denying heaven's spatial dimension altogether. Thus, one renowned New Testament scholar has written, 'We shall not expect, however, to find a description of a place, so much as the presence of a person.'[4]

Why is it necessary to insist on the geography of heaven as a location? One reason has to do with the current whereabouts of Jesus' resurrected body. When Jesus arose into the cloud above the Mount of Olives, the body was one which could be touched and handled. Jesus had underlined the point by eating fish with his disciples on a Galilean beach and saying to one of them that a ghost does not possess flesh and bones as he did. The ascension was clearly a signal that a corporeal body was being taken into heaven. Where did it go? Are we to believe that it disappeared into nothingness? And what about the case of Enoch, who was taken (bodily) into God's presence? (Gen. 5:24). Something similar happened to Elijah (2 Kings 2:11). And Paul tells us of an experience in which he was taken into the 'third heaven', and it was possible (though Paul is not certain about it) that he was taken there bodily (2 Cor. 12:1-4). Certainly, there was nothing in Paul's understanding of heaven that precluded the possibility that he might have been taken there bodily. On the contrary, everything about the New Testament's teaching about heaven leads us to expect that it is a place.

Heaven as we now think of it is a temporary mode of existence. What we look forward to is not the intermediate state (what happens to the soul at the point of death), but the final state (when the body will rise from the grave). That final condition, the new heavens and the new earth (2 Peter 3:13; Rev. 21:1-4), has to be material in nature. Man is corporeal. He is both body and soul. Christ restores what was lost due to sin. He restores us to what we were meant to be, a purified psychosomatic being created anew to live for God's glory for ever. The only way we can imagine it is after the pattern of what happened to Christ after his own death. Because he lives in resurrection power, we shall live also, in the same way. Because he lives in the power of an indestructible life, and because we are united to him, the power of the Holy Spirit which raised him from the dead will raise us up also (Rom. 6:8-10; Heb. 7:16). At a point when death seemed imminent, Paul seemed to draw strength from the prospect of a corporeal heaven for his tired and aching body: 'Our citizenship is in heaven. And we eagerly await a Saviour from there, the Lord Jesus Christ, who, by the power that enables him to bring everything under his control, will transform our lowly bodies so that they will be like his glorious body' (Phil. 3:20-21).

Paul knew the constant debilitating effect of a 'thorn in the flesh' (2 Cor. 12:7-9), which daily hampered his energies for the work of the kingdom. The day will come, he said to himself and others, when the lame will walk, the blind see, the deaf hear and the dead rise.

Second, it is not just a place, but *one especially reserved for God's people*. We are meant to gather more than just its spatial dimension. It is a place that has been prepared for us to inhabit. I have been invited to wedding receptions in hotels where I could barely afford to spend a single night! It is always a wonderful sight to see my name neatly written on a card placed on the table reserved especially for me. I am expected and the meal I am about to consume is free — to me at least, though not to my host. Jesus goes to 'prepare' a place for us. No one will arrive in heaven and find he or she is not expected. No one will find a sign saying, 'No vacancies'.

But we are not to think of it as a hotel either! Jesus refers to heaven as 'my Father's house'. It is our home! Going to heaven is like going home. The Authorized Version uses the word 'mansions', which is misleading (you cannot have mansions within a house!). It comes from the Latin Vulgate translation *mansiones* (*mansio* means a dwelling). Think of a manse and you will be along the right lines. It is a resting-place; there we come home after the toil and burden of travel in this world. In the words of the Negro spiritual, 'He's coming for to carry me home.' Thus, Matthew Henry could say, 'He whose head is in heaven need have no fear to put his feet into the grave.'[5]

Third, Jesus assures the disciples that *there are many resting-places*, 'sufficient,' says Calvin, 'for a great number'.[6] Were the disciples afraid that the kingdom would be too small for all of them to inhabit it? Were they guilty of diminishing the extent of God's love for sinners? Were they overshadowed by a narrowness that suggested to them that only a very small number would eventually be chosen to dwell with Jesus? They may, indeed, have been hostages to such views, but, as J. C. Ryle comments, 'There will be room for all believers and room for all sorts, for little saints as well as great ones, for the weakest believer as well as for the strongest. The feeblest child of God need not fear there will be no place for him. None will be shut out but impenitent and obstinate unbelievers.'[7]

2. Heaven is where Jesus is

Jesus promises to return and take his disciples away so that they might be 'with me' (John 14:3). But what are we to make of the expression: 'with me'? Reading through John's Gospel creates the impression that more is meant than sharing heaven together. Later, Jesus made it his prayer: 'Father, I want those you have given me to be with me…' (John 17:24). The preposition in 17:24 is *meta* which means 'in company with'. But the preposition here, in 14:3, is *pros* which means 'towards'. It is more than a static relationship; there is a movement involved. It is more than being beside Jesus, though that surely is a wonderful thought. There is a relationship implied. Our love will go to him and his to us. It is the same preposition that John uses in the opening prologue. In the beginning, Jesus was the Word and the Word was 'with' God (John 1:1). In the relationship of the Father and the Son within the Trinity there is a mutual movement in love of one towards the other.

A little-known theologian of the twelfth century, Richard of St Victor, wrote what is perhaps one of the most important

works on the Trinity. Though a Scot, he lived in the Abbey of
St Victor, near Paris. One of the questions which he took up
and pondered was: 'Why is God a Trinity rather than a solitary
individual?' He came to the conclusion that God is love and it
is in the nature of love to be outgoing and reciprocal. It takes
more than one to share love![8] The point seems simple enough,
but it is really quite profound. In the relationship of the Father
to the Son there is love, a love that is constantly responding to
the needs of the other.

Just as the Son, in heaven, is with the Father, in a relationship of mutual love and adoration, so we shall enjoy a similar
relationship with our Saviour.

In addition to saying that we shall be 'with' Jesus, our
Saviour adds, '... where I am'. At first this appears a tautology.
Is there a difference between 'with me' and 'where I am'? Yes!
What Jesus means is something much more than our translation to heaven. He prays: 'Father, I want those you have
given me to be with me...' And Jesus does not leave it there.
He goes on to explain what he means: 'to see my glory' (John
17:24). Jesus had promised them his peace (14:27; 16:33) and
his joy (15:11; 16:22). Now, in addition, he wants them to see
his glory also. To be where Jesus is means to be in the presence
of his glory. Now we see him only dimly, 'a poor reflection as
in a mirror' (1 Cor. 13:12). There we shall see him as he is (1
John 3:2). The transfigured humanity of Jesus will display the
glory of God shining in his face (2 Cor. 4:6). There is a sense
in which we shall be unable to take our eyes off the majesty of
his being. We shall be surrounded by the glory of God.

Jesus knows their troubled hearts, and the only way to fully
relieve the pain is to show them that the cross is a temporary
phenomenon. There is something beyond the cross, something
glorious and unimaginably beautiful. He wants their eyes to be
opened and to behold what lies in store, not only for Jesus, but

for them also. He also wants them to know that his prayer will
be answered. This is no idle wish on Jesus' part. The disciples
had been given to Christ in covenant. The bond that unites
them is sealed in his blood which is about to be shed on their
behalf. God's promises are inviolable, and prayers uttered in
order to fulfil a promise are the best kind of prayers. To pray,
'Lord, you promised!' is to be sure of success, and Jesus
intended them to catch its significance.

But there is one more thought. Not only shall we be in the
presence of glory. We shall share in the glory! That is what
Jesus goes on to pray: 'I have given them the glory that you
gave me...' (John 17:22). Jesus shares his glory with us! What
does that mean? He shares his image, his sonship, his inheritance, his throne! And this is mystery indeed. It is what Peter
means when he says, 'You ... participate in the divine nature'
(2 Peter 1:4).

And when will all this be? Jesus promises to come back for
them. In fact, the promise sounds very similar to another that
is made in the same chapter: 'I will not leave you as orphans;
I will come to you' (14:18). 'I will come back... I will come to
you.' Although the same verb is used in both cases, the
reference has in view two quite different occasions. In the first
instance, Jesus comes back in order to take his disciples away
with him. In the second instance, Jesus returns in order that the
disciples take him into their hearts. We have already noted that
what is in view in this second instance is the coming of the
Holy Spirit on the Day of Pentecost. He comes as Christ's
agent to dwell in the hearts of every disciple of Jesus. The
earlier promise is different. What is in view here is not
Pentecost, but the *Parousia*; not the coming of the Holy Spirit,
but the Second Coming of Christ.

At least, this is the prevailing understanding of these words.
Some commentators have suggested, however, that the language

is deliberately vague at this point. When Jesus suggests that he will return to take his disciples to be where he is, he may be referring to the disciples' own death. At that time they will be 'away from the body and at home with the Lord' (2 Cor. 5:8). Others have suggested that what is in view here is a deliberate echo of what Jesus will say later in this chapter, referring to his coming to them as the Holy Spirit is sent by him upon his return to the Father's right hand. It is true that the same word, 'rooms' (in John 14:2), is also found in verse 23, where it is translated 'home' and refers to the Spirit making his home in the hearts of believers. But it seems more likely that Jesus has in view, not just their spiritual presence with him after their death, or the spiritual presence of Jesus with them by means of the Holy Spirit dwelling in their hearts; rather, he is referring to their bodily presence with him in heaven.

The words in the upper room were meant to convey something of Jesus' lordship. What they saw before them was Jesus incarnate, the Servant of the Lord. But Jesus wants them to glimpse his glory. Christians who have caught the vision of Christ's lordship are emboldened. One such was the aged Bishop of Smyrna, Polycarp. He was eighty-six, but still full of zeal for the faith. He was charged with treason for refusing to recite the oath to Caesar, yet his oppressors were reluctant to harm him, partly due to his great age, but mainly because of the respect in which he was held by the people. Even when he was brought into the arena, attempts were made to spare him. They asked him once again to recite the oath, but to no avail. He refused to say, 'Caesar is Lord!'

Polycarp was asked to say something else. It was something to which he could readily agree: 'Away with the atheists!' That was all he had to say. Who were the atheists? According to Rome, they were all those, including Polycarp, who refused to sanction the emperor's divinity. But Polycarp could not leave the matter there. Agreeing to say, 'Away with the atheists,' he added, 'Eighty-six years have I served him, and he hath done me no wrong; how then can I blaspheme my King who saved me? *Iesus ho kurios.*' *Iesus ho kurios* (Jesus is Lord!) Polycarp was executed, but with the vision of glory to come that would make the suffering he endured seem light by comparison.

7.
The ministry of sympathy and intercession

The work of redemption is finished. The demands of the law have been met. The guilt of sin has been dealt with. Sinners can now be reconciled to God through faith in Jesus Christ. The death of Christ and his presentation of himself before his Father's throne are aspects of his priestly ministry which cannot be repeated: 'He sacrificed for their sins once for all when he offered himself' (Heb. 7:27). 'Nor did he enter heaven to offer himself again and again, the way the high priest enters the Most Holy Place every year with blood that is not his own. Then Christ would have had to suffer many times since the creation of the world. But now he has appeared once for all at the end of the ages to do away with sin by the sacrifice of himself' (Heb. 9:25-26).

What are the immediate benefits of Jesus' presence in heaven as far as we ourselves are concerned? Calvin mentions two. In the first place, atonement having been made for our sins, reconciliation with the Father is now possible. 'He turns the Father's eyes to his own righteousness to avert his gaze from our sins... He fills with grace and kindness the throne that for miserable sinners would otherwise have been filled with dread.'[1] In the second place, we are strengthened against the trials of this life by the realization that Christ is now a King upon his throne: 'Faith comprehends his might, in which reposes our strength, power, wealth and glorying against hell... He therefore sits on high, transfusing us with power, that he may quicken us to spiritual life, sanctify us by his Spirit, adorn his church with divers gifts of his grace, keep it safe from all harm by his protection, restrain the raging enemies of his cross and of our salvation by the strength of his hand, and finally hold all power in heaven and on earth. All this he does until he shall lay low all his enemies and complete the building of his church.'[2]

This strengthening and protecting ministry is actually performed by a continuation of an aspect of Jesus' priestly ministry in heaven: 'The Lord has sworn and will not change his mind: "You are a priest for ever"' (Heb 7:21). 'Because Jesus lives for ever, he has a permanent priesthood' (Heb. 7:24). There are two aspects of this ministry to be considered: the ministry of sympathy and the ministry of intercession.

The sympathy of Christ[3]

In considering the sympathy of Christ there are several sources to which we must turn.

1. Jesus' compassion portrayed in the Gospels

The Gospels, over and over again, refer to Jesus' 'compassion' in his dealings with people in need. It is the emotion most frequently attributed to him (Matt. 9:36; 20:34; Mark 1:41; 6:34; 8:2; 9:22; Luke 7:13). The word used to express it is thought to be unknown in classical Greek but was used by Greek-speaking Jews long before the days of the New Testament as they endeavoured to convey God's compassion as expressed in the pages of the Old Testament (Exod. 33:19; Deut. 13:17; 28:54; 30:3; 32:36; etc.). This was the word the

Gospel writers used to describe how moved Jesus was by the sight of human distress. Thus his heart went out in compassion to a man with leprosy (Mark 1:41); to two blind men on the outskirts of Jericho (Matt. 20:34); to a distressed woman in Nain whose son had just died (Luke 7:13); to a great crowd of thousands who were evidently hungry (Matt 14:14; 15:32; Mark 6:34; 8:2); and to great numbers of sick and diseased folk (Matt 9:36).

Behind these situations of human grief and tragedy lay a spiritual poverty that caused our Lord's heart to overflow with compassion. They were 'like sheep without a shepherd' (Mark 6:34).

And his compassion was more than just an inward response; it showed itself in visible actions of tenderness and love. Thus, on hearing the news of the death of his friend Lazarus, and the evident grief of Mary, Lazarus' sister, Jesus wept silent tears (John 11:35). On another occasion, beholding something of the spiritual darkness of Jerusalem, his grief was more audible: 'As he approached Jerusalem and saw the city, he wept over it' (Luke 19:41). When a man, who was both deaf and dumb, was brought to him, Jesus uttered 'a deep sigh'. Significantly, that sigh was a prayer to his Father in heaven as Jesus 'looked up to heaven' and said, ' *"Ephphatha!"* (which means, "Be opened!")' (Mark 7:34). Every prayer which Jesus makes is filled with a compassionate sigh as he empathizes with our pain. And when such compassion was spurned, as in the case of the Pharisees, Jesus 'sighed deeply' (Mark 8:12). Such determined opposition to his every overture of love made him sore to the very bottom of his heart. It is one of the most poignant things in the Bible that Jesus is unfolded before our eyes as one moved with compassion towards the victims of sin's rage and hostility. In the face of death and bereavement especially, he was moved to tears.

Jane Crewdson's hymn expresses it exactly:

There is no sorrow, Lord, too light
To bring in pray'r to thee;
There is no anxious care too slight
To wake thy sympathy.

Thou, who hast trod the thorny road,
Wilt share each small distress;
The love which bore the greater load
Will not refuse the less.

There is no secret sigh we breathe,
But meets thine ear divine;
And ev'ry cross grows light beneath
The shadow, Lord, of thine.

Life's ills without, sin's strife within,
The heart would overflow,
But for that love which died for sin,
That love which wept with woe.

Whilst this word 'compassion' is used in Matthew, Mark and Luke, it never occurs in John. John's great word was, of course, 'love'. To the end of his days John urged the congregation in Ephesus to love one another as Christ had loved them. In the upper room, Jesus spoke of his love for the disciples: 'Greater love has no one than this, that he lay down his life for his friends' (John 15:13). What greater way is there for Jesus to show us his love than to call us his friends? Nowhere is this better illustrated than when Lazarus is described as 'the one you love' (John 11:3). And when he confronted Mary in her distress at the loss of her brother, Jesus was 'deeply moved in spirit and troubled' (John 11:33). Then again the apostle John himself is referred to on several occasions as 'the disciple whom Jesus loved' (John 13:23; 19:26; 20:2; 21:7,20).

2. *His intercession on our behalf*

We have already noticed that in promising the Holy Spirit Jesus was identifying his own ministry with that of 'another Counsellor' who would come in his place. By calling the Spirit '*another* Counsellor' Jesus is implying that he is himself a counsellor, though the only actual reference to him as Counsellor (advocate, *paraclete*) is in 1 John 2:1. It is John's expression for one aspect of the priestly ministry of Jesus: 'We have an Advocate with the Father, Jesus Christ the righteous' (1 John 2:1, NKJV). The word 'advocate' (*parakletos* in Greek) is expanded by the New International Version: 'We have one who speaks to the Father in our defence.' Jesus is the one in heaven who comes to our aid when we find ourselves in any trouble (just as the Holy Spirit comes to our aid in our own hearts!). Just as Jesus was moved with compassion at the sight of the ravages of sin upon his disciples during his earthly ministry, so now, in heaven, he springs to the defence of all who find themselves harassed in any way.

3. *The temptations of Christ*

There is specific reference to the sympathy of Christ, exercised in his ongoing capacity as High Priest, from his present location at God's right hand. The book of Hebrews, more than any other book in the New Testament, emphasizes Jesus' role as High Priest (Heb. 2:17; 3:1; 4:14). But we are not to understand this in terms of someone who is distant and aloof from our situation. Jesus' present ministry draws from the wealth of experience gained during his incarnate life. 'Because he himself suffered when he was tempted, he is able to help those who are being tempted' (Heb. 2:18). 'For we do not have a high priest who is unable to sympathize with our weaknesses, but we have one who has been tempted in every way, just as we are — yet was without sin' (Heb. 4:15). Jesus is able both to sympathize and to help us in our trouble because he has himself been the victim of temptation. Indeed, at the very outset of his public ministry, Jesus was 'sent' into the desert to be tempted by Satan *by the Holy Spirit*. He had come to declare war on the ministry of principalities and powers. The victory of Christ was in defeating the devil's power. 'The reason the Son of God appeared was to destroy the devil's work' (1 John 3:8).

Jesus was tempted throughout his life; from the cradle to the grave he was the subject of Satan's particular interest. But we are given glimpses during the course of his life of instances whereby Satan made him the object of intense provocation. There are the hours in Gethsemane where his commitment was tested, almost to breaking-point. The intensity (desirability) of the temptation to be spared the cross is shown in both word and deed. The bloody perspiration indicated the physical trauma. And the cry revealed how close to the bone Satan had managed to get: '"My Father, if it is possible, may this cup be taken from me. Yet not as I will, but as you will"' (Matt. 26:39).

Another occasion occurs at the very beginning of Jesus' public ministry, in the wilderness of Judea (Matt. 4:1-11). There are several features of this temptation which are important to grasp.

First of all, it is crucial that *Christ is not depicted merely as a victim*; he was *driven* into the wilderness by the Holy Spirit (Matt. 4:1). Mark is more graphic still: using the verb *ekballei,* he suggests that Jesus was impelled to go and meet the devil (Mark 1:12). The initiative is God's. It is at once a declaration of war against the powers of darkness.

Secondly, *Jesus is represented as the Last Adam*. The entire setting reminds us of the story of Eden. The forbidden fruit of the garden had three main attractions: 'good for food ... pleasing to the eye ... desirable for gaining wisdom' (Gen.

3:6). Likewise, Jesus encountered three specific temptations. In addition, Luke, in his account, places the temptation narrative immediately following the genealogy of Jesus, and the preceding verse links his ancestry (according to the flesh) with Adam (Luke 3:38; 4:1). Where Adam failed, Jesus succeeded.

Thirdly, *the purpose behind Satan's grand design is an attempt to circumvent the fulfilment of doom-laden prophecy in the opening pages of the Bible.* Satan knows that the coming of Christ spelled his downfall: the seed of the woman would crush the head of Satan (Gen. 3:15). His aim throughout was to tempt Christ to fulfil his role as Messiah without a cross. The temptation was real: the prophecy had contained a warning that the Messiah himself would be bruised in the process. But the Servant-Jesus insists on stamping upon the serpent, taking no regard for the pain it inflicts on himself.

The temptation to turn stones into bread after a period of prolonged fasting was real enough. But had Jesus done so, he would have ceased to be man's representative. He would no longer be able to stand next to us and say, 'I know what it's like to suffer hunger. I know what it's like to wait on the Lord to provide for my needs.' That was the lesson Israel had to learn in the wilderness. They were placed in a position whereby they had to trust God for daily provision (the manna). Jesus must ask for bread in God's time, like we do.

To jump from the temple pinnacle into the valley below in the expectation that angels would prevent his body from being damaged, was, Satan implied, what Psalm 91 was all about:

> He who dwells in the shelter of the Most High
>   will rest in the shadow of the Almighty.
> I will say of the Lord, "He is my refuge and my fortress,
>   my God, in whom I trust." ...
> For he will command his angels concerning you
>   to guard you in all your ways;

they will lift you up in their hands,
  so that you will not strike your foot against a stone'
                                                    (Ps. 91:1-2,11-12).

It all sounds plausible enough for the Son of God. But had he done so, it would have been an indication that he needed some kind of demonstration of God's love. It would have been testing God, as though Jesus had been in doubt of his care. Jesus must trust his Father continually, on a moment-by-moment basis. Jumping off the pinnacle would have been a theatrical stunt, something that by its very essence would need to be repeated over and over each time providence placed him in difficult circumstances.

The third temptation sees Jesus on a high mountain being offered the kingdoms of the world by Satan. Satan was lying, of course. The kingdoms are not his to give. He 'is a liar and the father of lies' (John 8:44). Jesus had already been promised the kingdoms of the world by his Father in heaven (Ps. 2:8; Dan. 7:14). Whatever Satan thought he had to offer Jesus, it was nothing. To have received it would have been an act of short-sightedness, gaining a shabby crown with no cross. Jesus had come to worship God. Apart from his Father in heaven, all is futile and vanity.

That Jesus repelled Satan's temptations goes without saying; but this was not accomplished without sustained and powerful effort on Jesus' part. In the desert, the battle was preceded by a long fast. At Caesarea Philippi, when Peter was used by Satan as a mouthpiece, the Lord's rebuke was sharp — 'Get behind me, Satan!' (Mark 8:33) — suggesting that a raw nerve might have been touched (Satan was, after all, suggesting the lie that he need not be crucified to accomplish his aims). And in Gethsemane his 'sweat was like drops of blood falling to the ground' (Luke 22:44). We are led to understand that, on the eve of his death, Jesus met the full onslaught of Satan, an encounter which required all of his resources to repel.

How Christ ministers his compassion to us

Throughout Jesus' ministry, then, we are made aware of his compassion. It is a compassion that springs from a life which has known the bitterness of temptation, but has refused to yield. How does Jesus exercise this ministry to us? We shall consider two aspects in particular:

1. He opens up Scripture to us. It is important to note that Jesus met the onslaughts of Satan by the sword of Scripture. He noticed that the three chapters in Deuteronomy recalling the experience of Israel in the wilderness (Deut. 6-8) were peculiarly relevant to his own situation. Likewise, he ministers to us his compassion by opening up the Scripture to our troubled hearts. This is what he did for two tired, dejected disciples on the Emmaus road (Luke 24:13-35). There are circumstances which seem beyond explanation, too raw, too fierce to reconcile; but Scripture will reveal that a greater purpose is at stake than just our ease. In the Bible study on the road to Emmaus, the eyes of these two disciples were opened to behold God's plan of redemption, a plan which had to include the horrors they had witnessed at Calvary just two days before. These precious truths were the antidote for the poison of sorrow.

As Spurgeon once preached, 'There is in the Bible a remedy exactly fitted for your grief if you could only find it. Sometimes you lose the key of a drawer, and you must have it opened, and therefore you send for the whitesmith [i.e. one who works in metal goods] and he comes with a bunch of keys. Somewhere among them he will have a key that will open your drawer. The Bible contains keys that will open the iron gates of your trouble, and give you freedom from your sorrow.'[4]

2. He gives strength in trouble. At other times, Jesus' compassion is by imparting supplies of strength in times of trouble. There is, at the very heart of a cyclone, a spot where all is calm. Christians can testify to a ministry of peace, of an inner calm, when all about them is raging. When Paul and Silas sang psalms in a Philippian prison, they were testifying to this very experience. When Peter was brought before the magistrates after Pentecost, he testified to being 'filled with the Holy Spirit' (Acts 4:8). He had been filled only a few days earlier, and now was filled again. It was, of course, a fulfilment of what Jesus had promised: 'When you are brought before synagogues, rulers and authorities, do not worry about how you will defend yourselves or what you will say' (Luke 12:11). By yielding ourselves up to God and his ministry of compassion, we can know and feel a sense of repose even in the face of raging storm.

Intercession

The New Testament only alludes to Christ's continuing intercession on behalf of his people on two specific occasions: 'Who is he that condemns? Christ Jesus, who died — more than that, who was raised to life — is at the right hand of God and is also interceding for us' (Rom. 8:34). 'Therefore he is able to save completely those who come to God through him, because he always lives to intercede for them' (Heb. 7:25). The testimony of these two references, however, is clear enough: Jesus continues to offer petitions to his Father on our behalf.

As to what precisely Jesus says in fulfilment of this ministry, this is best seen by an examination of an example of such ministry witnessed *before* his ascension in John 17. David

Chrytaus at the time of the Reformation first referred to it as the 'high-priestly prayer' of Jesus, and the title has stuck ever since. Hebrews 5:1-2 outlines the necessary qualifications in a high priest. He must:

> be chosen by God;
> be consecrated to the service of God;
> share in the weakness of those he represents;
> be concerned about the needs of others.

All these requirements are clearly seen in John 17:

> The authority Jesus possessed was given to him by the Father (v. 2).
> 'I sanctify myself' (v. 19), Jesus said, expressing his devotion to the Father's will.
> Jesus knew the weakness of his brethren, having just earlier been 'troubled in spirit' (13:21) and here asking that he be once again glorified (v. 5).
> John 17 is a prayer
> > for himself (vv. 1-5);
> > for his disciples (vv. 6-19);
> > for all the people of God (vv. 20-26).

The Master at prayer

How does Jesus pray?

He prays with conviction. There is something quite different about John 17 from the prayer recorded in Gethsemane. In the olive garden, Jesus fell to the ground and said, 'My Father, if it is possible, may this cup be taken from me' (Matt. 26:39). In

John 17 it is quite different: 'Father, I will that they also, whom thou hast given me, be with me where I am; that they may behold my glory' (John 17:24, AV).[5] In the upper room, it is not so much, 'If it is possible...' but 'I will...' The difference in tone is noticeable. In fact, this prayer in the upper room is one which only Jesus could pray. It is not so much a request as a demand. His will is identical to his Father's. In Gethsemane, all the emphasis falls on Jesus as the Servant of God. He is taking our sins upon himself and the thought of it is overwhelming. It is something from which he would wish to recoil, if another way of fulfilling his mission were possible. But such a way cannot be found, and it is eloquent of the Saviour's submissiveness to his Father's will that he bows in compliance. In John 17 it is different. He prays in the assurance of his identity as the Son of God, an identity that is deepened by the conviction that the Father loved him 'before the creation of the world' (17:24). The knowledge of their communion together as Father and Son enhances the conviction that he has a right to ask whatever he wills, knowing that his will conforms to that of his Father in heaven.

For whom does Jesus pray?

As Divine Mediator, he intercedes only for his own. He does not pray for all: 'I am not praying for the world' (17:9). Specifically, he prays for those whom the Father has given to him (17:2,9,11,12,24; cf. 6:37,39,65; 10:25-30). Those for whom he prays are the elect. And it is noteworthy that election is no barrier to prayer for Jesus; rather, it is an incentive! Several things ought to follow:

1. The knowledge that we are the Father's love-gift to the Son, and therefore the most precious thing Jesus

possesses, is *comforting*. Nothing strengthens like the
knowledge that we are loved by someone — by
Someone!

2. The knowledge that we are not only loved, but
continuously prayed for is *ennobling*. We meditate too
little on the truth that God cares for us. 'Your Father
knows what you need before you ask him,' Jesus says
(Matt. 6:8). Peter, possibly after discovering the truth
afresh, urges his readers to 'Cast all your anxiety upon
him because he cares for you' (1 Peter 5:7). We are those
for whom Jesus cares.

3. The knowledge that Jesus intercedes on the basis
of an assured divine relationship is *steadying*. Our lives
are subject to all kinds of disruptive forces that threaten
to undo us. But our present relationship to God is one
that will not be severed. On the contrary, it will develop
and grow. What we are now is not what we are going to
be. If we are children, we are heirs — heirs of God and
co-heirs with Christ (Rom. 8:17). Jesus assures us that
he has lost none (John 17:12).

For what does Jesus pray?

Here, we can only summarize the exact focus of Jesus'
intercession in the upper room. There appear to be five main
concerns.

First, *he prays that his disciples might be protected* (John
17:11). We need to be clear that Jesus does not pray that his
disciples might be kept free from trouble of any kind. Suffering is part and parcel of following Jesus, of being 'in the
world'. We are co-heirs of Christ 'if indeed we share in his
sufferings' (Rom. 8:17). What Jesus prays for is our persever-
ance. Satan has desired to have us, but Jesus has prayed for us!
(cf. Luke 22:31-32).

Second, *he prays that we might have joy* (John 17:13). As the answer to first question of the *Shorter Catechism* expresses it, we are meant 'to glorify God and enjoy him for ever'. Resolute atheist that he was, it is not surprising that the poet P. B. Shelley (1792-1822) could write:

> Rarely, rarely, comest thou,
> Spirit of Delight.

But it is tragic that Christians also experience far too little of the joy that comes from knowing God through Jesus Christ. Joy is what we were made for, and what we are meant to know.

Third, *he prays for the church's unity.* Three times Jesus stresses it: the church on earth ought to be united: 'that all of them may be one' (17:21); 'that they may be one as we are one' (17:22); 'May they be brought to complete unity' (17:23). Thomas Manton puts it forcibly: 'This prayer is a standing monument of Christ's affection to the Church.'[6] What kind of unity does Jesus have in mind? It is a unity in the faith: 'through their [the apostles'] message' (17:20). Each subsequent generation of disciples is to believe the same truths as the apostles believed. It is to be a unity in the truth. It is also a unity modelled after the pattern of that which exists between the Father and the Son: 'that all of them may be one ... just as you are in me and I am in you' (17:21). Clearly, since Jesus goes on to suggest that the world will be influenced by such a display of unity, what he has in mind must be outward and tangible. It must be a unity not only of doctrine and truth, but also life and character. The goal of all that Jesus has accomplished is our sanctification.

Fourth, *he wills that we may be with him* (17:24). This had been the burden of his ministry that evening. He was going ahead of them to make ready for them the many rooms in his Father's house. He wants us to share his home and his triumph.

It is, says Thomas Manton, his last will and testament. 'When
Jesus made his will, heaven is one of the legacies which he
bequeathed to us. This was his last will and testament, "Father,
I will." Heaven is ours, a legacy left us by Christ.'[7]

Fifth, *he wants them to see his glory.* The disciples had
already received his glory in words and actions. But Jesus
wants them to see him as he really is. Just as an athlete will
beckon to his family after winning a race so that they might
join in the triumph, so Jesus wills that, having seen his
humiliation, they should now see something of his glory in the
only place where it can be seen — heaven! 'Now we see but
a poor reflection as in a mirror; then we shall see face to face'
(1 Cor. 13:12).

> Face to face with Christ my Saviour,
> Face to face — what will it be
> When with rapture I behold him,
> Jesus Christ who died for me?
>
> Face to face shall I behold him
> Far beyond the starry sky;
> Face to face in all his glory,
> I shall see him by and by!
>
> F. A. Breck

One of the consequences of being with Christ and beholding his glory is that we shall be like him — perfectly sanctified
and free from sin. Clearly, a transformation is required. 'For
those God foreknew he also predestined to be conformed to the
likeness of his Son, that he might be the firstborn among many
brothers' (Rom. 8:29). 'Dear friends, now we are children of
God, and what we will be has not yet been made known. But
we know that when he appears, we shall be like him, for we
shall see him as he is' (1 John 3:2).

Finish, then, thy new creation;
Pure and spotless let us be:
Let us see thy great salvation
Perfectly restored in thee;
Changed from glory into glory,
Till in heaven we take our place,
Till we cast our crowns before thee,
Lost in wonder love and praise.

Charles Wesley[8]

What we have been examining is an example of Jesus' high-priestly intercession on behalf of his own that has been given to us from the days of his humiliation. It is the burden of Romans 8:34 and Hebrews 7:25 that such a ministry continues in heaven. Various objections have been raised against the idea. Does it not call into question the lordship of Christ that he is placed in a position of one who must solicit from his Father? Or, to ask the question from another perspective, does it not call into question the love of the Father for us that he must needs be asked?

John Murray has eloquently answered the objection: 'Divine exigencies required that redemption should have been wrought through mediation of the Son, and it only enhances our view of the knowledge, love and beneficence of the Father to discover the economy in terms of which he brought to fruition the designs of his love. And, as far as the exaltation of Christ is concerned and the sovereignty he exercises by reason of that exaltation, we must not forget that it is an economical exaltation. It is one awarded to him because he took the form of a servant and was obedient unto death, even the death of the cross. And if it is an economical exaltation, it is an exaltation that does not suspend economical arrangements. There is a continuity between that phase of the process of redemption which is complete and the phase that is still unfolding itself. It is a patent fact written in the boldest fashion on the New Testament witness that the mediation of Christ is not suspended and the intercession is but one concrete aspect of that mediation.'[9]

As Christians we may rest assured that every moment of our lives is superintended by the ever-watchful eye of our Saviour, who lives for the very purpose of ensuring our protection and eventual glorification. The doctrine of Christ's ascension is calculated to bring us the most comfort and to challenge us to live in the light of its truth.

8.
Watching for the return of our Lord

First, a parable: a man is preparing to leave for an indefinite
period. He gathers his servants together and gives to each one
a suitable task to perform in his absence. The night-watch-
man's task is obvious enough. He must stay awake during the
night to guard the property. To sleep when on duty would be
a serious offence. When the master of the house returns, he
must make sure that he is awake.

Being vigilant for the Lord's return is a theme that the Bible
seems eager to emphasize. Jesus has ascended to his Father's
throne as King and Head of the church. From this location he
distributes gifts to the church and intercedes on their behalf.
But one day, he is coming back. Though the Bible contains
some things which are hard to understand, there is one prediction which stands out clear and certain, namely the promise
that the Lord Jesus Christ will come again. Indeed, the New
Testament contains references to Christ's return in every one
of its twenty-seven books except Galatians and the short
epistles, Philemon and 2 and 3 John.

Three important words capture the significance of the
Lord's return. The word most frequently used to describe the
event is *parousia* (e.g. 1 Cor. 15:23; 1 Thess. 2:19; 3:13; 4:15;
5:23), which in secular Greek denoted the visit of the emperor

or some such distinguished person. A literal translation might come up with something like 'being nearby', and has associated with it the idea of approaching and a sense of presence. For example, Paul writes of the pleasure which the advent (the *parousia*) of Titus gave him (2 Cor. 7:6-7). In the same way, and with even greater anticipation, we are to expect the coming of our Saviour from heaven.

The second word is *epiphaneia* (which is only to be found in Paul's letters, e.g. 2 Thess. 2:8; 1 Tim. 6:14; 2 Tim. 4:1,8; Titus 2:13). This is a general word and means 'appearing'. Paul also uses this word to describe Jesus' first coming (2 Tim. 1:10). Christ's second appearance will be as real and historical as was his appearance in Bethlehem.

The third word, which is also sometimes translated as a 'revelation', is *apokalupsis* (1 Cor. 1:7; 2 Thess. 1:7; 1 Peter 1:7,13). The idea behind this word is of an event that is at present hidden, but will in due course be unveiled to human view. Taking all three words together, we have the idea of Christ's presence after a period of absence *(parousia)*, the shining of his glory after his humiliation *(epiphaneia)*, and the unveiling of his majesty and power *(apokalupsis)*.

Such is the centrality of the Second Coming of Jesus Christ in the New Testament that a reference to it is recorded in the formula recited each time we celebrate the Lord's Supper: in it the Lord's death is proclaimed 'until he comes' (1 Cor. 11:26). At the end of his first Corinthian epistle, Paul adds an Aramaic expression *Marana tha*, 'Come, O Lord!' (1 Cor. 16:22). And the last book of the Bible begins and ends with an eye on the coming of Christ: 'Look, he is coming with the clouds, and every eye will see him... Amen. Come, Lord Jesus' (Rev. 1:7; 22:20).

Jesus is coming again. That he is coming *again* throws an emphasis on the fact that he has already come. And as we read our Bibles we find that we are to consider both aspects of the Saviour's coming and hold them together. When we use the word 'eschatology' — which literally means 'talk about last things' — we are not to think exclusively about Jesus Christ's return.

Take a glance at any textbook on theology and you will probably discover that the discussion on eschatology comes at the end of the book, with little and sometimes no reference at all to anything else in the book. Many Christians feel, as a consequence, that life can be safely lived without too much thought given to 'the end', particularly if we are likely to have died by the time Jesus Christ returns. 'Eschatology', then, is for the specialist Christian. Of course, nothing could be further from the truth.

Back to the future!

In the Bible, eschatology is just as much about the present as it is about the end. Reading the Gospels teaches us to think of the Bible's view of the end in terms of Christ's first coming, as well as his second coming.

Jesus preached 'the good news of the kingdom' (Matt. 4:23). Something new had dawned with the first coming of Christ that had only been anticipated before. When the disciples heard Jesus preaching and witnessed the miracles that he performed they were witnessing something which the prophets and godly folk of the Old Testament period had longed to see but didn't (Matt. 13:11,16-17). 'All the Prophets and the Law prophesied until John [the Baptist],' who was the last in a long line of men who prepared the way for the coming of Christ as the Messiah. Since that time 'the kingdom of heaven has been forcefully advancing' (Matt. 11:12-13). At the return of Jesus Christ, the kingdom — which even now is present and advancing — will be fully realized. Hence, Jesus taught us our most basic prayer: 'Your kingdom come' (Matt. 6:10).

The beginning of the end

From the start of Jesus' ministry, we get the impression that we are to understand that we are living in a world that is heading towards 'the end', that as Christians we live in 'the last days'. God has spoken to us in his Son 'in these last days' (Heb. 1:2). Jesus' death on the cross took place 'at the end of the ages' (Heb. 9:26). Jesus Christ has appeared as our perfect sacrifice 'in these last times' (1 Peter 1:20). And every opposition we face as the Lord's people is an opposition of antichrist(s) — an evil force that was already present in the apostle's day as well as something which will manifest itself at the time of Christ's second coming (1 John 2:18).

Something quite extraordinary occurred at the first coming of Christ: the end was ushered in. Though it is not often understood in this way, this is what Paul means when he says that Christ's first coming occurred 'when the time had fully come' (Gal. 4:4). Something new occurred when Jesus came into the world: history as the world knew it came to an end, and the process which leads to the final curtain coming down was inaugurated. When Paul speaks about the resurrection of Christ in that magnificent chapter of 1 Corinthians 15, he speaks of it in terms of what it means for us who believe: the resurrection of Christ is 'the firstfruits of those who have fallen asleep' (v. 20). The 'firstfruits' were a promise of a harvest to follow. Christ's resurrection was an indication that an entire harvest of resurrections is going to follow. His rising has ensured the beginning of the end.

Living with the end in view

Knowing that we live in the 'last days', that eschatology does not merely refer to something in the far and distant future, has profound implications for the way we are to live our lives. In a passage that is sometimes not fully understood (in the same way as Galatians 4:4 quoted above), Paul tells the Corinthians that if any anyone is 'in Christ, he is a new creation; the old has gone, the new has come' (2 Cor. 5:17). As a Christian I belong to a new and different order of creation. Scripture looks forward to a day when all that was originally meant to be will come to pass. The fall of man, with all of its frustration and decay, will be put right. Paul anticipates this on a cosmic scale when he says, 'The whole creation has been groaning as in the pains of childbirth right up to the present time' (Rom. 8:22). But what birth is creation expecting? Paul has just explained: 'The creation was subjected to frustration, not by its own choice, but by the will of the one who subjected it, in hope that the creation itself will be liberated from its bondage to decay and brought into the glorious freedom of the children of God' (Rom. 8:20-21). And the point is that there are signs that this has already begun. Jesus' coming, and especially his resurrection, was a sign that it has already started. The resurrection of Jesus Christ is the first sign of springtime, and the guarantee of a final harvest.

One of the things we can confidently expect at the end is what the *Shorter Catechism* refers to as an 'acquittal'.[1] How is that? Because we are here and now justified by faith alone in Jesus Christ alone. Our present justification is part and parcel of what we mean by eschatology. Talk about 'last things' must not be relegated to the last chapter of a book with no reference to what I am now experiencing. We have already 'crossed over from death to life' (John 5:24). Resurrection life is something we have now, even though we may die (John 11:25-26).

This has the most profound consequences as we struggle with sin. We are to tell ourselves that we are much more than what we see reflected in a mirror. 'Do not let sin reign in your mortal body... Do not offer the parts of your body to sin, as instruments of wickedness,' Paul urges. And what resources are there to call on to help me resist the temptations of sin? Supremely, this one: you are those 'who have been brought from death to life' (Rom. 6:12-13). You are different! You belong to a different world-order now! Resurrection life flows through you. There is no greater incentive to holiness than a reminder of who we really are, and where we are heading for.

In particular, two things are true of me as a Christian: sin lives in me (Rom. 7:17), and at the same time 'Christ lives in me' (Gal. 2:20). Christ lives in me by his Holy Spirit, who is referred to as 'deposit' on our inheritance (Eph. 1:14) and the 'firstfruits' of our harvest (Rom. 8:23). The gift of the Holy Spirit is like having a little of the future — now! Eschatology, then, teaches us to live now with the future in mind. If Christ is my Master, and heaven my ultimate home, then sin has to be evicted. We are to show sin no mercy. If we want to keep our way pure then we shall have to be careful not to walk where our shoes can pick up dirt. Living with our 'mind on things above', that is, on the kingdom which has already begun and will one day be completed, will help us live as we ought. This is living eschatologically! Nothing could be more practical than that!

Back to the parable! Jesus is coming again — soon! It will be sooner than we often think. Are you waiting, ready, pre-pared? In a sermon on the need to be watchful for the Lord's return, J. C. Ryle exhorted: 'Let us live as if His glory was concerned in our behaviour. Let us live as if every slip and fall was a reflection on the honour of our King. Let us live as if every allowed sin was one more thorn in His head, one more nail in His feet, one more spear in His side. Oh! let us exercise a godly jealousy over thoughts, words, and actions; over motives, manners, and walk. Never, never let us fear being too strict. Never, never let us think we can watch too much.' And then citing the last words of a dying Christian, Ryle adds: 'Brother, brother, we are none of us more than half awake!'[2] Too true!

Notes

Preface
1. Caspar Olevianus, *A Firm Foundation,* translated and edited by Lyle D. Bierma (Baker Book House, 1995), p.78.
2. John Calvin, *Commentary upon the Acts of the Apostles* (Baker Book House, 1981), commentary on Acts 1:9.
3. From the hymn, 'With glorious clouds encompassed round...'

Chapter 1
1. Calvin, *Acts,* vol. XVIII, p.43.
2. John Chrysostom, *Homily II,* p.14.
3. See J. I. Packer, *Knowing Christianity* (Eagle, 1995), p.190.
4. Calvin, *Acts,* p.59.
5. John Calvin, *Institutes of the Christian Religion,* ed. J. T. McNeill, trans. F. L. Battles (Westminster Press, 1960), II.xvi.14.

Chapter 2
1. Calvin amplified on earlier patristic formulations which spoke of Christ's work as King and Priest (which he had used in early editions of the *Institutes*), adding a third concept, that of his work as Prophet (which he adopted in his final edition of the *Institutes* of 1559). This threefold office of Christ, the so-called *munus triplex,* was to dominate Reformed theological formulations of Christ's work thereafter.
2. John Murray, *Collected Writings of John Murray,* 'The Heavenly, Priestly Activity of Christ' (Banner of Truth Trust, 1976), vol. 1, p.48.
3. That is to say, Jesus rendered his obedience both passively and actively.
4. Apart, that is, from the New American Standard Version. Other translations, including the AV, have used 'covenant' elsewhere in this chapter.

5. Thus the plural in verse 17, a covenant is in force only *over dead bodies* (only one body is required to validate a last will and testament), and the verse goes on to say, 'It never takes effect while the one who made it is living.' This last verse has been conclusive to most readers that the writer is talking in terms of a last will and testament, the provisions of which are not generally distributed until the testator dies. But this is incorrect on two counts. First, some wills are made, the terms of which become effective immediately, whilst the testator is still alive. Such wills from the Ancient Near East are known to have been made. Second, the writer is not talking about distribution but validation, and a will becomes valid as soon as it is made!

In addition, the section reads as one logical argument. There is a close connection between each of the verses from 16 through to 18: 'In the case of ... because ... this is why...' Since the word means 'covenant' in verse 18, it must have the same meaning in verses 16-17. For these reasons, it is best to understand these verses as referring to a covenant. In the case of a covenant it is ratified (lit.) 'over the dead'; for a covenant to be 'in force' (lit. 'to make firm, binding'), or to 'take effect' (lit. 'to make strong') it is necessary to prove the death of the covenant-maker (in this case symbolically in the presence of animal victims). God is saying he is as good as dead if he fails to keep his pledged, covenanted, word.

6. The death of one man does not in itself forgive the transgression of another man. Testamentary deaths are not substitutionary. Jesus' death, however, was substitutionary; the covenantal nature of his death ensured that he died for the sake of others.

7. Sinclair B. Ferguson, *A Heart for God* (Banner of Truth Trust, 1987), p.46.

8. Thus, the Revised Standard Version: 'He entered once for all into the Holy Place taking not the blood of goats and calves but *his own blood*, thus securing an eternal redemption' (emphasis added).

9. In addition to the argument presented in the text, this view is misguided for the following reasons: first, in order to maintain the typology, it is insisted upon that since the high priest carried the blood in separation from himself into the Holy of Holies, Christ must do the same. Whilst this is true in part, the typology cannot be pressed that far, since the high priest was not himself devoid of blood as he carried the blood of sacrifice into the Holy of Holies. Second, it is difficult to maintain that Jesus remains human in his glorified condition if his body is bloodless. True, he did speak to the disciples in one of the resurrection appearances of his body as being composed of 'flesh and bones' rather than 'flesh and blood' (Luke 24:39).

But to press this into suggesting that his body had no blood seems a step too far. Third, the verse in question, Hebrews 9:12, does not contain a verb indicating that he took his blood with him. He entered *(dia)* 'on account of', or 'through' his blood. He entered not *in order to secure* our redemption, but as one who had *already secured it.*

10. Philip E. Hughes, *A Commentary on the Epistle to the Hebrews* (Eerdmans, 1977), p.338.

11. From the hymn, 'Look ye saints! The sight is glorious.'

Chapter 3

1. C. S. Lewis, *The Last Battle* (Lions, Harper-Collins, 1980), p.132.

2. Packer, *Knowing Christianity,* p.189.

3. Commenting on the expression 'he learned obedience' in Hebrews 5:8, Calvin wrote, 'The first purpose of the sufferings of Christ was that in this way He should be made accustomed to obedience: not that He was forcibly compelled to it, or had any need of such practices, in the way that the fierceness of oxen or horses is tamed. He was more than willing of His own accord to give the Father the obedience due to him' (*The Epistle of Paul the Apostle to the Hebrews and The First and Second Epistles of St Peter,* trans. William B. Johnston, eds D. W. and T. F. Torrance (Wm B. Eerdmans, 1963) pp.65-6).

In addition, Calvin was to write: 'Now someone asks, How has Christ abolished sin, banished the separation between us and God, and acquired righteousness to render God favourable and kindly toward us? To this we can in general reply that he has achieved this for us by the whole course of his obedience' (*Institutes,* II.xvi.5).

4. See the terminology used in Answer 22 of the *Shorter Catechism.*

5. John Calvin, *A Harmony of the Gospels: Matthew, Mark and Luke,* ed. D. W. Torrance and T. F. Torrance, trans. A. W. Morrison (St Andrews Press, 1972), vol. III, p.151.

6. From the hymn, 'Hark! The herald angels sing.'

7. Donald Macleod, *The Humiliated and Exalted Lord,* ed. J. Ligon Duncan III (Reformed Academic Press, 1994) p.21.

8. For this interpretation, see Moisés Silva, *Philippians, The Wycliffe Exegetical Commentary,* ed. Kenneth Barker (Moody Press, 1988), p.132.

9. It is true that Jesus was called 'Lord' during his incarnate life, but in many of these instances the title is used in the vocative as a form of polite address (e.g. Matt. 15:27; 18:21) and means something equivalent to our English, 'Sir'. It is the equivalent of the Hebrew 'Rabbi'. But there are occasions when Jesus used the title 'Lord' about himself, investing it with

all the connotations of deity. One such passage is Mark 12:35-40, where Jesus reminds worshippers in the temple courts that David had prophesied in Psalm 110 that the Christ (Messiah) would be David's 'son' and David's 'Lord' at the same time. This particular psalm is crucial, for it led the early church to think of Jesus as Lord. And it is also true that following his resurrection, Thomas used the same title, with the same divine connotation when, having been asked to reach out his hand and physically examine Jesus' body for the evidence of a real resurrection body, he exclaimed, 'My Lord and my God!' (John 20:28).

10. John Calvin, commentary on Philippians 2:11.

Chapter 4

1. George Smeaton, *The Doctrine of the Holy Spirit* (Banner of Truth Trust, 1961), p.126.

2. Hugh Martin, *The Abiding Presence* (Knox Press, n.d.), p.104.

3. The illustration is Jim Packer's. See J. I. Packer, *Keep in Step With the Spirit* (Inter Varsity Press, 1984), p.66.

4. See D. A. Carson, *The Gospel According to John* (Inter Varsity Press, 1991), p.322.

5. John Murray, *Redemption — Accomplished and Applied* (Banner of Truth Trust, 1961), p.161.

6. Sinclair Ferguson, 'The Death of Sin/The Way of Life,' in *Inside the Sermon,* edited by R. A. Bodey (Baker Book House, 1991), p.89.

7. *Ibid.,* p.113.

8. Murray, *Redemption — Accomplished and Applied,* p.163.

Chapter 5

1. This is the view taken by D. M. Lloyd-Jones. See *Christian Unity: An Exposition of Ephesians 4:1-16* (Banner of Truth Trust, 1980), pp.199-200.

2. A technical defence of this view can be found in Andrew Lincoln's commentary on Ephesians — *Ephesians, Word Biblical Commentary* (Word Books, 1990), pp.253-4; cf. C. Hodge, *A Commentary on the Epistle to the Ephesians* (originally published 1856, reprinted Banner of Truth Trust, 1964), p.229.

3. For a defence of this view, see William Hendriksen, *Ephesians* (Banner of Truth Trust, 1967), p.198.

4. J. I. Packer, *Keep In Step With the Spirit* (Inter Varsity Press, 1984), p. 83.

5. The finest defence of this view can be found in O. Palmer Robertson's *The Final Word: A Biblical Response to the Case for Tongues and Prophecy Today* (Banner of Truth Trust, 1993).

6. Robertson, *The Final Word,* pp.75-7.

Chapter 6

1. It is best read as an imperative, 'Trust in God...', rather than as an indicative, 'You do trust in God...'

2. J. C. Ryle, *Expository Thoughts on the Gospels, St John* (James Clarke & Co. Ltd, 1976), vol. III, p.55.

3. J. Gresham Machen, *Christianity and Liberalism* (Victory Press, 1923), p.81.

4. Donald Guthrie, *New Testament Theology* (Inter Varsity Press, 1981), p.875.

5. Quoted by John Blanchard, *Gathered Gold* (Evangelical Press, 1984), p.58.

6. John Calvin, *Commentary on the Gospel According to John.*

7. Ryle, *Expository Thoughts on John,* p.57.

8. Richard de St Victor, *De Trinitate: texte critique avec introduction notes et tables,* edited by Jean Ribaillier (Paris, 1958). Book 3, *The Trinity,* is available in English in *The Classics of Western Spirituality,* 'Richard of St Victor'. Translation and introduction by Grover A. Zinn (Paulist Press, 1979).

Chapter 7

1. Calvin, *Institutes,* II.xvi.16.

2. *Ibid.*

3. See B. B. Warfield, 'The Emotional Life of our Lord' in *The Person and Work of Christ* (Presbyterian and Reformed Publishing Company, 1970), pp. 93-145; John Murray, 'The Heavenly, Priestly Activity of Christ' in *Collected Writings of John Murray* (Banner of Truth Trust, 1976), vol.1, pp. 44-58.

4. C. H. Spurgeon, *Metropolitan Tabernacle Pulpit* (Pilgrim Publications, 1974), vol. 33, p.418.

5. The weaker translations of the verb used here, *thelo,* 'I want' (NIV), and 'I desire' (NKJV) need not be set at odds with the stronger 'I will' of the Authorized Version. Hendriksen insists that 'This type of desiring is not weaker than willing' (*John, New Testament Commentary,* Banner of Truth Trust, 1954, p.366).

6. Thomas Manton, *An Exposition of John 17* (Sovereign Grace Book Club, 1958), p.9.
7. *Ibid.,* p.92.
8. From the hymn, 'Love Divine, all loves excelling'.
9. Murray, *Redemption — Accomplished and Applied,* p.53.

Chapter 8
1. *Shorter Catechism,* Answer 38.
2. From a sermon by J. C. Ryle entitled 'Watch!' published by Hunt & Son, 'Caledonian' Steam Press, Ipswich, p.31.